25 Ways to Sew Jelly Rolls
Layer Cakes & Charm Packs

BRIONI GREENBERG

D&C

David and Charles

www.stitchcraftcreate.co.uk

CONTENTS

INTRODUCTION

I love pre-cuts and have hoarded them for years. The magpie in me just can't help being drawn to those pretty little packages of fabric. As their name suggests, pre-cuts are pieces of fabric that have already been cut into sizes suitable for use in patchwork and quilting and are a great way of getting a small sample of all the prints in a range when you have neither have the money nor the inclination to buy acreage, or for new quilters who haven't yet accumulated a fabric stash.

My guess is that many of us have pre-cuts hoarded in cupboards and are unwilling to use them because they look so lovely, and daren't spoil them by unravelling them (we all know that once that ribbon has been taken off it is impossible to get a pre-cut rolled up and perfect looking again). But, trust me, you will love them even more once you have created something gorgeous from them!

This book contains 25 projects designed to inspire you to get those little bundles of loveliness used up. There are even projects to use up those last few jelly roll strips and charm squares so that you get to squeeze every last bit of enjoyment out of them.

There are purposely no difficulty ratings in this book. Those of you who have already quilted before don't need them and the last thing the newer quilters amongst you need is someone telling you what they think you're capable of. The first book I ever bought had no difficulty ratings either. The first two quilts I ever made from that book were a cathedral window quilt and one with inset seams, on the naïve assumption that I could pull them off. People often comment that I have a fearless approach to quilting but, to me, the quilts were in the book so of course they were possible, right? Right.

Pick the design you like, get your fabric at the ready and go for it. Don't be put off by any of the projects as some look more complex than they actually are. What's the worse that can happen? You may have to unpick a couple of seams or go and buy a little more fabric, but the satisfaction of making something gorgeous from your precious pre-cuts is priceless. And if you don't get it perfect, the quilt police are not going to come knocking at your door.

I hope you enjoy making these projects as much as I did!

HOW TO USE THIS BOOK

Whether you are new to quilting and want to buy some fabric for a quilt without breaking the bank, or you are a seasoned quilter with more pre-cuts in your stash than you know what to do with and need some inspiration, this is a quintessential guide to using pre-cuts.

This book contains projects made with many of the common pre-cuts on the market. I have also used a variety of techniques to complete the 12 quilts and 13 small projects.

I have created a table of the pre-cuts used in this book so that you can see at a glance which pre-cuts each project uses. Have you seen some charm packs that you adore? Have you seen some jelly rolls on sale at a price you can't refuse? Have you got three jelly rolls and a charm pack in your stash and you don't know what the heck to do with them? Simply look at the table below to get a quick view of which projects you can use them for without having to read the fabric requirements for each and every project. The table also specifies where you need background fabric or supplementary pre-cuts or yardage.

The pre-cut requirements for the projects are shown with flower symbols; I have also indicated with small stars which other pre-cuts could be used for the same project. Using the guide to the yield of each piece in Cutting Your Own Pre-cuts, it is simple enough to convert one pre-cut to another.

Once you have chosen your project, the requirements list on each pattern page will detail any additional requirements for binding, backing or linings.

	FOCUS FABRIC								BACKGROUND/ SUPPLEMENTARY FABRIC				
	MINI CHARM SQUARES	CHARM SQUARES	JELLY ROLL	LAYER CAKE	FAT EIGHTH	FAT QUARTER	DESSERT ROLL	SCRAPS	CHARM PACK	JELLY ROLL	LAYER CAKE	FAT QUARTER	YARDAGE
SUMMER PETALS			✿				★	★	✿				
CIRCLES SQUARED				✿							✿		
FLOWER GARDEN			✿				★	★					✿
CRISS-CROSS PATCHES		✿		★			★		✿		★		★
MERRY-GO-ROUND			✿				★						✿
PRETTY PINWHEELS		✿	✿				★			✿			
TWIRLING WINDMILL					✿	★							
SQUARE ROOT	★		✿				★	★		✿			
CONTRAFLOW				★	✿	★	★				★		✿
SHURIKEN		★	✿								✿		
STARS AND STRIPES			✿				★						✿
GIANT'S CAUSEWAY				★	✿		★						✿
EASY PEASY PLACE MATS		★			✿	★	★						
WINTERBERRY TABLE RUNNER					✿	★							✿
DASHER BATHMAT			✿				★	★			★	✿	✿
BIG AND BOLD CIRCLES CUSHION			✿			★					✿		
JAUNTY BUTTON-DOWN IPAD CASE	★	✿										✿	
STARBURST TOTE BAG			✿				★						✿
GERBERA BAG CHARM		✿	✿										
FAIRYTALE PINS'N'THINGS	✿	★	★	★				★					✿
YOYO LANYARD AND CARD HOLDER		✿	✿					★					
HEXAGON FLOWERS NOTEBOOK		✿				✿		★		★			
VERDANT SEWING MACHINE COVER		✿					★	✿					✿
QUIRKY CUBE BAG	★	★	✿				★			★		✿	
CHEERFUL CARRIER		✿		★		★	★	★		★			✿

ABOUT PRE-CUTS

'Pre-cuts' is the general term applied to those lovely little bundles of fabric found in quilting and fabric shops tied up with pretty ribbon. They come in all shapes and sizes but the most common ones found in quilting shops are charm packs which contain 5in (12.7cm) squares, jelly rolls which contain strips that are 2½in (6.3cm) wide that are as long as the width of the fabric (typically 44in/111.8cm), and fat quarter bundles which contain varying numbers of fat quarters.

For those of you who have never heard the term 'fat quarter' before, it refers to the way the fabric is cut. If you bought a quarter of yard/metre of fabric off the roll you would be buying a piece of fabric that is a quarter of a yard/metre in length and the whole width of the fabric (typically 9in x 44in/22.9cm x 111.8cm). A fat quarter refers to a quarter of a yard or metre that is cut by literally cutting the yard/metre into four quarters, so it would measure half a yard/metre long, and half the width of the fabric (typically 18in x 22in/45.7cm x 55.9cm) in length. Fat quarters on the whole tend to be more versatile than long quarters.

There are many fabric manufacturers who supply pre-cuts. The ones that produce the largest range are probably Moda and Robert Kaufman but Westminster, Riley Blake, Hoffman, Timeless Treasures, Art Gallery Fabrics and most other quilting

fabric manufacturers also now produce them in various forms. There are also many quilting shops that put together their own pre-cuts and bundles. Ask at your local quilt store to see whether they do.

There are many different names for pre-cuts and the numbers of fabric pieces contained within each varies between manufacturers so bear this in mind when you are looking for them. The number of fabric pieces required for each pattern is also detailed in the individual patterns so double check the pre-cut you plan to use to ensure that you have enough fabric to complete the project!

The various names and the number of pieces contained within each pre-cut is detailed here:

2½in (6.3cm) squares
Mini charm pack - 42 squares

5in (12.7cm) squares
Charm pack – 30, 40 or 42 squares
Bali snaps – 40 squares
Mini Tonga treat – 40 squares
5in (12.7cm) stacker – 1 of each print in the fabric line

2½in (6.3cm) strips x the whole width of the fabric
Jelly roll - 40 strips
Design roll – 30 strips
Roll up - 42 strips
Bali pops - 40 strips
Tonga treat strips - 40 squares
Rolie polie - 1 of each print in the fabric line

10in (25.4cm) squares
Layer cake - 42 squares
Ten squares - 42 squares
Tonga treat squares - 40 squares
Bali crackers - 40 squares
10" stacker - 1 of each print in the fabric line

5in 12.7cm) strips x the whole width of the fabric
Dessert roll - 20 strips

9in x 21in (22.9cm x 53.3cm) – an eighth of a yard
Fat eighth bundle – generally 1 of each print in the fabric line

18in x 21in (45.7cm x 53.3cm) – a quarter of a yard
Fat quarter bundle - generally 1 of each print in the fabric line

CUTTING YOUR OWN PRE-CUTS

There are many manufacturers that produce pre-cuts but what if your favourite line of fabric is from one that doesn't? The answer is to make your own.

All of these pre-cuts can be cut from your scraps, but here is the quantity you can cut from other pre-cuts and yardage.

Charm square - 5in x 5in (12.7cm x 12.7cm):
4 mini charm squares (2½in x 2½in/5cm x 5cm)

Layer cake square - 10in x 10in (25.4cm x 25.4cm):
16 mini charm squares

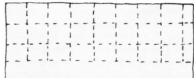

4 charm squares

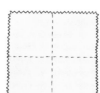

Fat eighth - 9in x 22in (22.9cm x 55.9cm):
24 mini charm squares

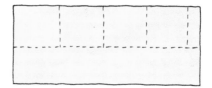

4 charm squares

Fat quarter – 18in x 22in (45.7cm x 55.9cm):
56 mini charm squares

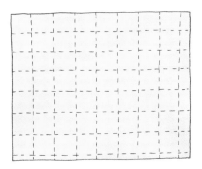

12 charm squares

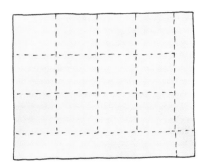

2 layer cake squares

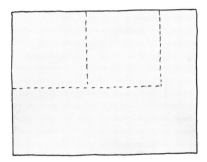

Long quarter (yard) – 9in x 44in (22.9cm x 111.8cm):
51 mini charm squares

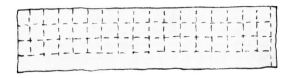

8 charm squares

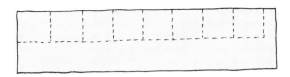

3 jelly roll strips (2½ in x 44in/6.3cm x 111.8cm)

½ yard (0.4m) – 18in x 44in (45.7cm x 111.8cm):
24 charm squares

1 yard (0.9m) – 36in x 44in (91.4cm x 111.8cm):
56 charm squares

7 jelly roll strips

14 jelly roll strips

4 layer cake squares

12 layer cake squares

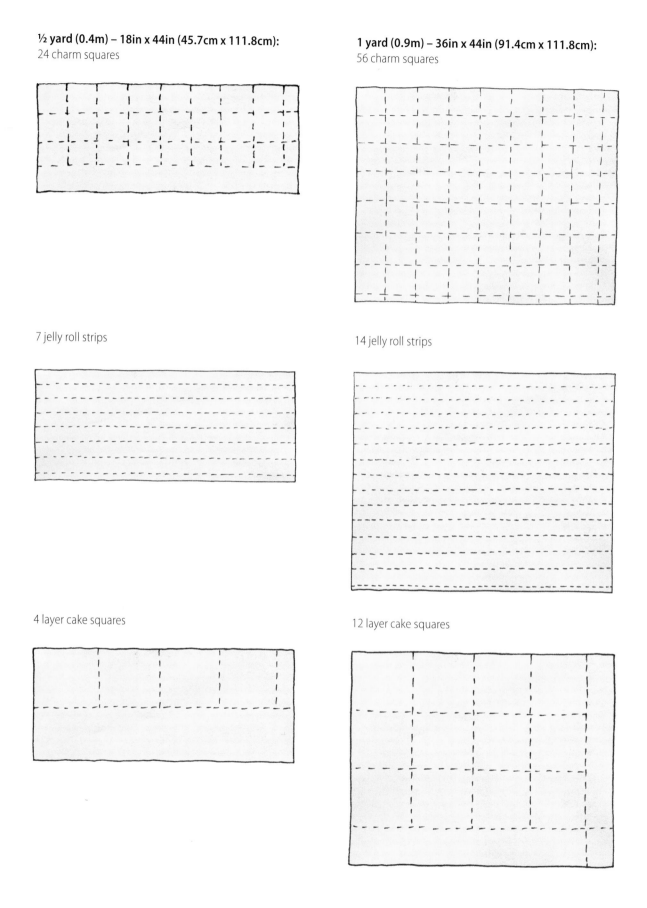

TIPS FOR USING PRE-CUTS

Size

The smaller pre-cuts, such as mini charm packs, charm packs, jelly roll strips and layer cakes, are most commonly cut with a pinked edge (zigzag). There are a couple of things to note. The size of the pinking varies massively between manufacturers. Some are tiny and some are as big as 2–3mm from the top to the bottom.

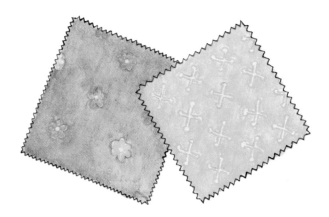

Also, the size of the cut pieces can vary ever so slightly between manufacturers, batches or fabric lines. Some measure the width or length to the bottom of the pinking and some to the tips of the pinking.

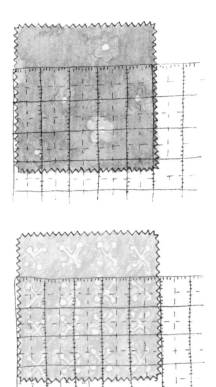

As accuracy in your sewing is key to getting your seams to match up, it is worth measuring them before you start to establish how yours are cut so you can take account of this when you are sewing the pieces together. This is particularly important when you are joining a pre-cut piece to a piece you have cut from yardage.

Pre-wash or not

Whether you pre-wash your fabrics in general is largely personal preference; however, it is important that you do not wash pre-cuts as they have been cut accurately to a very specific size.

The shrinkage rates between different manufacturers and even different fabric lines from the same manufacturer can differ widely. Washing will shrink the fabric slightly. Sometimes if the fabric has been printed with the grain of the fabric not completely straight, washing will straighten the grain, so you are likely to end up with pieces that are smaller than you want them to be and in some cases slightly distorted.

I am a huge fan of pre-washing but I steer well clear when using pre-cuts!

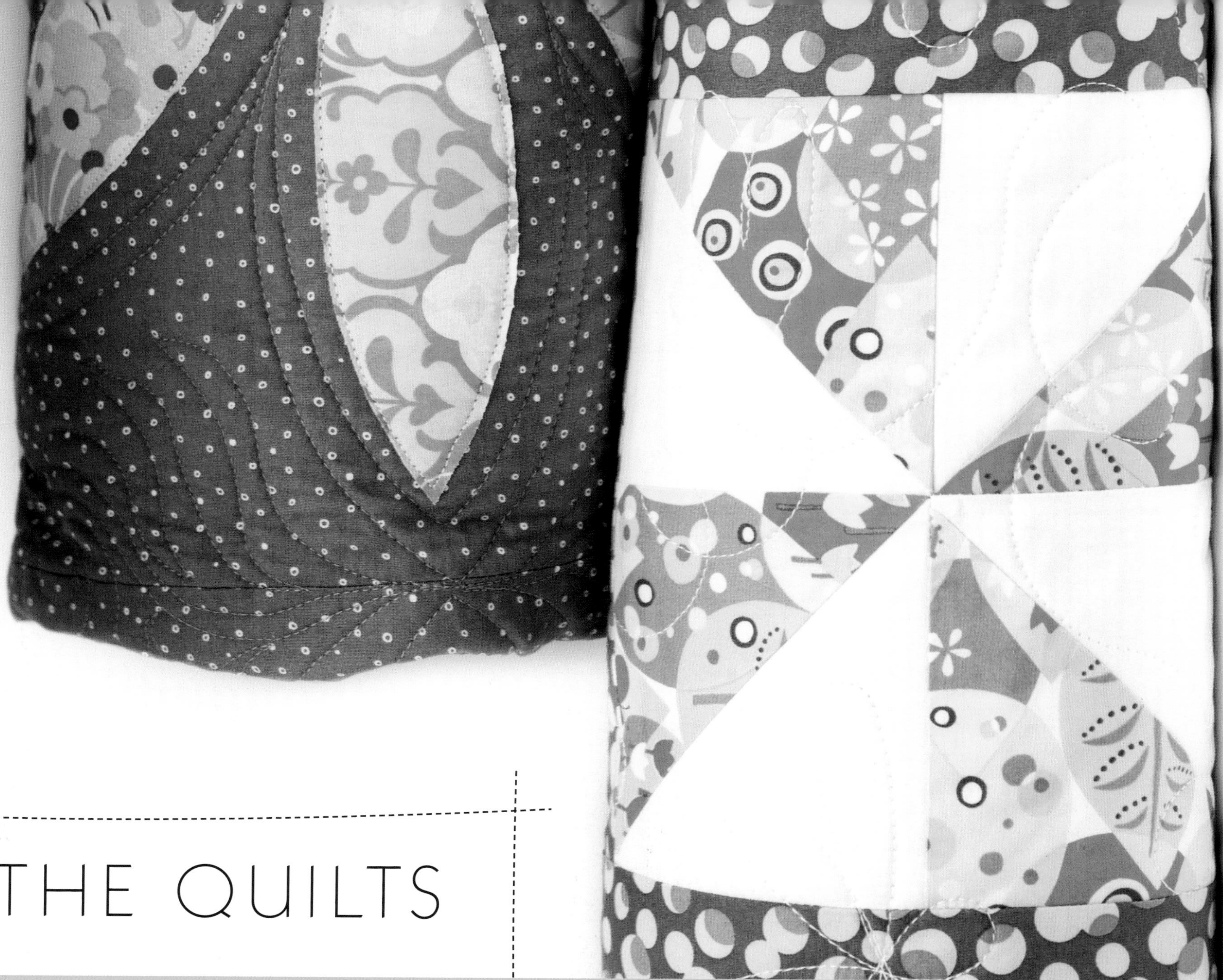

THE QUILTS

SUMMER PETALS

SIZE: 76in x 102in
(193cm x 259cm)

THIS pretty quilt, with its repeating pattern of brightly coloured petals on a light background, captures the feel of summer perfectly and would instantly brighten a plain bedroom.

- 2 jelly rolls (71 strips)
- 10 charm packs for background (I used 5 white and 5 cream and alternated the squares to create a chequerboard effect)
- 6 yards (5.5m) of fabric for backing
- ⅔ yard (0.6m) of fabric for binding
- Piece of wadding (batting) at least 82in x 108in (208.3cm x 274.3cm)
- 5–6 yards (4.6–5.5m) of fusible web, 36in (91.4cm) wide

1 PREPARING AND CUTTING FABRICS

From the jelly roll strips choose 71 strips for the petals.

From the charm packs cut 76 rectangles, 2½in x 5in (6.3cm x 12.7cm); and four squares, 2½in x 2½in (6.3cm x 6.3cm). If you are using two colours for the background, you need to ensure that you cut out half of one colour and half of the other. Leave the rest of the charm squares as they are.

From the fusible web cut 83 strips, 2½in x 36in (6.3cm x 91.4cm). Cross-cut 12 of these strips into 6in (15.2cm) lengths.

From the binding fabric cut nine strips, 2½in (6.3cm) x the width of the fabric. Remove all selvages.

From the backing fabric cut two pieces approximately 42in x 72in (106.7cm x 182.9cm). Remove all selvages.

2 PREPARING THE LEAVES

Cut the fusible web into 2½in (6.3cm) strips. Following the manufacturer's instructions, press the fusible web strips, paper side up, on to the back of each jelly roll strip. The fusible web generally comes in widths of 35in (88.9cm) so you will need one full strip and some of a second strip for each.

Using the template and the diagram as a guide, draw the petals on to the paper side of the fusible web, butting them up to each other. Cut out all the petals following the drawn lines. You should have 2816 petals in total.

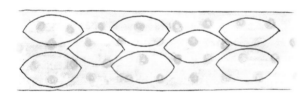

3 PREPARING THE BLOCKS

For each block take a charm square, fold it in half and press. Fold the square in half again and press. You should finish up with a triangle.

Press the folded piece with a hot iron, ensuring that creases are formed on all edges. Open the fabric out and the fabric piece should look like this.

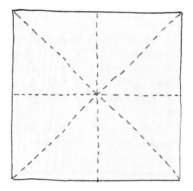

Choose eight petals, remove the paper backing from each, and place them on the background fabric so that the inside points of each of the petals are about the same distance from the centre as each other, and the ends of the petals are no less that ⅜in (0.9cm) from the edge of the charm square.

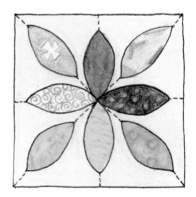

Once you have placed all eight petals and are happy with them, gently press the petals until they are all securely adhered to the background fabric.

The next step is dependent on how you plan to do your quilting. If you are planning to quilt an all-over pattern, you need first to sew around the edge of the petals to attach them permanently to the background squares. If you wish to do this, sew around the edge of every piece approximately ⅛in (0.3cm) in from the edge of each piece.

If you plan to quilt sympathetically to the design, you can leave the petals unattached for the moment and stitch them down as part of your quilting.

TIP

So that you do not have to remove the pieces again once you have positioned them, remove all backing papers from all petals before you start.

4 ASSEMBLING THE TOP

Lay out the blocks until you are happy with the placement. Sew each strip of blocks together and press the seams.

Once each row is joined, sew the rows together until the quilt top is complete. Press the seams as you go along.

5 MAKING AND ADDING THE BORDER

To make the two side border pieces, sew 22 of the 2½in x 5in (6.3cm x 12.7cm) charm rectangles together end to end. You should have two strips that measure 99½in (252.7cm) long. Sew one of these to each side of the quilt. Press seams outwards.

For each of the two top and bottom border pieces, sew 16 of the 2½in x 5in (6.3cm x 12.7cm) charm square rectangles together end to end. To each end of the strips, sew a 2½in x 2½in (6.3cm x 6.3cm) square. You should now have two strips that measure 76½in (194.3cm) long. Sew these to the top and the bottom of the quilt. Press seams outwards.

TIP

If wish to stitch the petals down as part of the quilting, make sure they are well pressed down so that they stay stuck until the piece is fully quilted.

6 PREPARING THE BACKING

Sew the 108in (274.3cm) lengths of fabric together to form a piece measuring approximately 86in x 108in (218.4cm x 274.3cm).

7 FINISHING

Layer up the backing, wadding (batting) and quilt top and baste using your chosen method.

Start quilting from the centre and work your way out to the edges.

Join all the binding strips together and press the seams. Fold the binding strip in half lengthways and press. Join the binding to the front of the quilt using a ¼in (0.6cm) seam and join the ends. Hand stitch the binding down to the back of the quilt.

TEMPLATE
Shown at 100%

CIRCLES SQUARED

SIZE: 60in x 60in
(152.4cm x 152.4cm)

ALTHOUGH this patchwork pattern of interlocking circles looks complicated it is in fact easier than it appears. Using a rotary cutter will give you identical shapes that will fit together perfectly.

YOU WILL NEED

- 1 layer cake piece of print fabric (32 squares)

- 1 layer cake piece of contrasting background fabric (32 squares)

- 3¾ yards (3.4m) of fabric for backing

- ½ yard (0.4m) of fabric for binding

- Piece of wadding (batting) at least 66in x 66in (167.6cm x 167.6cm) square

- Template plastic or cardboard (optional)

- Jenny Pedigo curved ruler (optional)

1 CUTTING FABRICS

From the layer cake pieces of both the print fabric and background fabric cut all 64 pieces in half diagonally.

From the binding fabric cut six strips, 2½in (6.3cm) x width of fabric.

From the backing fabric cut two pieces, 66in (167.6cm) x width of fabric.

TIP

Two layer cakes, one each of print and background fabric, would give you enough pieces to make a co-ordinating circles cushion. If you wish to make the cushion too, sew all 80 layer cake pieces following the instructions up to the end of Step 2 and put 16 blocks aside for later.

2 CUTTING CURVED PIECES

Lay each triangle of layer cake on the cutting mat, lining up the edges with the markings on the cutting mat.

If you wish to use the template, lay the template on the triangle, mark the curves on the fabric and cut along the marked lines. Keep all the pieces.

If you are using the curved ruler, lay the ruler on the fabric so that the 3½in (8.9cm) line on the ruler lines up with the long edge and the curve is centred on the triangle.

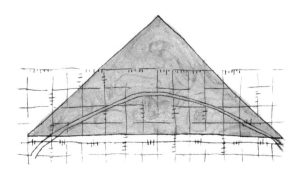

Using a rotary cutter, cut along the curve of the ruler. If you are using the ruler, the cuts will not quite reach the edges so just snip through each end of the curve with sharp scissors. Keep all the pieces.

3 MAKING THE BASIC BLOCKS

Each block is made up of an outer section and an inner curve. Opposite quarters of each block have a print fabric outer section, and a background fabric inner section while the other quarters have a background fabric outer section and a print fabric inner section.

Take an outer section and an inner section and fold them in half. Finger press both on the centre line and open.

Lay the inner section on top of the outer section, aligning the centre pressed lines. Sew a ¼in (0.6cm) seam from the centre to the edge, ensuring that you do not stretch the fabrics. Repeat for the other side of the block. Carefully press the seam towards the curve, ensuring that you do not distort or stretch the pieces.

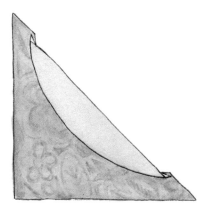

Lay the half-block on your cutting mat aligned with the markings.

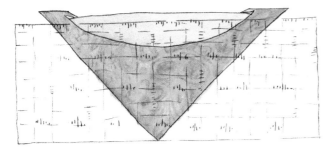

Trim the half-block so that the widest point of the curve measures 1¾in (4.4cm). Complete this step for all half-blocks.

Sew the two corresponding half-blocks together and press the seams open to reduce bulk. Complete this step for all blocks.

TIP

I find that a light spray of starch before pressing adds stability to the blocks. It also makes them much flatter and easier to trim.

4 STACKING AND CUTTING THE BLOCKS

Take two blocks and lay one on top of the other so that the side of the block with a plain fabric background is laid on top of a block that has a print fabric background. Ensure that the seams are lined up and pin together.

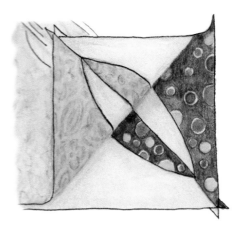

Take your ruler and draw a line from one corner to the other so that the line intersects the curve. Using a ¼in (0.6cm) seam, sew a line in from both sides of the drawn line.

Cut the block diagonally in half down the drawn line. Press the seams open. Complete this for all 64 blocks.

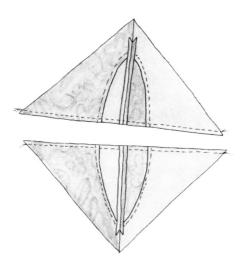

5 ASSEMBLING THE LARGE BLOCKS

Lay out four blocks using the photograph as a guide. The background sections of the blocks should be together and the print portion of the blocks should be together. Once you are happy with the placement, sew the four blocks together and press the seams. Complete this for the rest of the blocks until you have 16 blocks, each made up of four small blocks.

6 ASSEMBLING THE TOP

Lay out the 16 large blocks, positioning the blocks using the photograph as a guide. Once you are happy with the placement, sew the blocks together into rows, and then sew the rows together. Press the seams as you go along.

TIP

Ensure that where the blocks are joined together the print fabric sections of the block are sewn to a print section, and a background fabric sections are sewn to a background section. It's easy to get them the wrong way round by mistake.

7 PREPARING THE BACKING

Take the two pieces of backing fabric and sew them together so you have a piece measuring approximately 66in x 82in (167.6cm x 208.3cm).

8 FINISHING

Layer up the backing, wadding (batting) and quilt top and baste using your chosen method.

Start quilting from the centre and work your way out to the edges.

Join all the binding strips together and press the seams. Fold the binding strip in half lengthways and press. Join the binding to the front of the quilt using a ¼in (0.6cm) seam. Hand stitch the binding down to the back of the quilt.

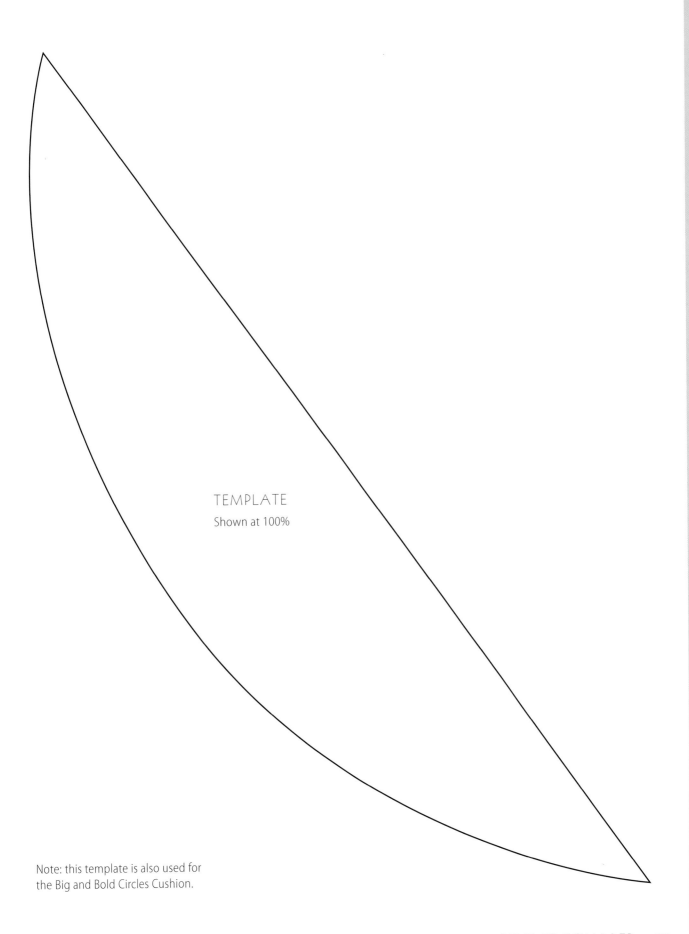

TEMPLATE
Shown at 100%

Note: this template is also used for
the Big and Bold Circles Cushion.

FLOWER GARDEN

SIZE: 78in x 78in
(198.1cm x 198.1cm) square

THE design of this pretty quilt incorporates simple stylized flowers, which are raw-edge appliquéd on to a dark background fabric. The use of yellows and greens creates the effect of a sunny flowery garden.

- 1 jelly roll (24 strips)
- 1 charm pack (32 squares)
- 4¼ yards (3.9m) of fabric for background
- 4½ yards (4.1m) of fabric for backing
- Piece of wadding (batting) at least 81in (205.7cm) square
- 4½ yards (4.1m) of fusible web, 17½in (44.4cm) wide

1 CUTTING AND PREPARING FABRICS

From the jelly roll strips choose 16 for petals and eight for the border. From these strips cut eight strips, 19in (48.2cm) long, and four squares, 2½in x 2½in (6.3cm x 6.3cm).

From the background fabric cut 16 squares, 19in x 19in (48.3cm x 48.3cm).

From the charm squares choose 32 for flower centres and motifs.

From the backing fabric cut two pieces, 81in (205.7cm) x width of fabric and two pieces, 84in (213.4cm) x width of fabric. Remove all selvages.

From the fusible web cut 36 strips, 2½in (6.3cm) long; 18 strips, 2½in x 5in (6.3cm x 12.7cm); and 32 squares, 4½in x 4½in (11.4cm x 11.4cm).

2 PREPARING THE FLOWER PETALS

Using the manufacturer's instructions, press two 17½in (44.4cm) long fusible web strips and one 5in (12.7cm) strip paper side up on to the back of 16 jelly roll strips.

Using template A and the diagram as a guide, draw the petals on to the paper side of the fusible web, butting them up as closely as possible to each other. You should get eight petals from each jelly roll strip.

Cut out all petals following the drawn lines. You should have 16 groups of eight petals.

4 PREPARING THE BACKGROUND FABRIC

For each block take a 19in (48.2cm) square of background fabric, fold it in half and press. Fold the square in half again and press. Then, fold in half on the diagonal, so you finish up with a triangle. Press the folded piece with a hot iron, ensuring that a crease is formed on all edges. Open the fabric out and the fabric piece should look like this.

3 PREPARING THE FLOWER CENTRES AND MOTIFS

Using the manufacturer's instructions, press the 4½in (11.4cm) fusible web squares paper side up on to the back of the 32 charm squares. Using template B, draw the centre circles on to the paper side of the fusible web and in the centre of each circle draw the small flower using template C.

Cut out all circles and flowers following the drawn lines. You should have 32 circles and 32 flowers in total. Take six circles and six flowers and cut them in half to make 12 halves. Take one circle and one flower and cut them in half and half again to make a total of four quarters.

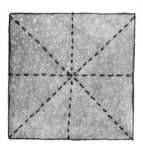

Take a set of eight petals and place them on the background fabric with the points of the petals lining up with the pressed lines. Place a centre circle into the centre of the block and adjust the placement of the petals so that none of the inner points of the petals are visible in the centre of the circle. Place a small flower in the centre.

Once you have placed all the pieces and are happy with the placement of them, press following the manufacturer's instructions until all pieces are adhered firmly to the background fabric. Complete all 16 blocks in the same way.

The next step is dependent on how you plan to quilt this and there are two options. If you are planning to quilt the finished quilt with an all-over pattern then you need to sew around the edge of the petals first to attach them permanently to the background squares. To do this, sew around the edge of every piece approximately ⅛in (0.3cm) in from the edge. If you plan to quilt sympathetically to the design then you can leave these unattached for the moment and stitch them down as part of your quilting.

5 ASSEMBLING THE TOP

Lay the blocks out in rows of four until you are happy with the placement. Join each strip of blocks together with a ¼in (0.6cm) seam and press the seams open. Once each row is joined, sew the rows together until the quilt top is complete. Press the seams open as you go along.

TIP

Once you have laid out your blocks and are happy with the placement, take a photograph and view the layout on your camera screen. Sometimes a smaller image enables you to spot blocks that may need switching.

6 ADDING THE MOTIFS

In the corners where four blocks join, place a centre circle and adjust the placement so that the point where the four seams meet is in the centre of the circle. Then place a small flower in the centre. Once you are happy with the placement of the motifs, press until all pieces are adhered firmly to the background fabric.

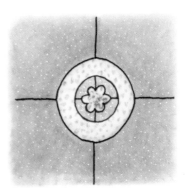

To add the half-motifs around the edge of the quilt, place a semi-circle on the quilt so that its flat edge is against the quilt edge and the seam runs down the centre of the circle. Then place a small half-flower in the centre, again lining the flat edge up with the edge of the quilt. Press until all pieces are adhered firmly to the background fabric. Complete this for all edges where two blocks meet.

To complete the top, place the quarter-circles and flowers on the corners of the quilt and attach as below.

TIP

The more control you have when free motion quilting the better. To help increase your control, draw some shapes on to waste fabric, layer up with wadding (batting) and some more waste fabric and practise quilting along your drawn lines. Remember that practice makes perfect!

7 PREPARING AND ADDING THE BORDER

Sew the 19in (48.2cm) jelly roll strips together end to end into groups of four. You will then have four lengths that each measure 74½in (189.2cm) long. On to each end of two of these strips sew one of the 2½in x 2½in (6.3cm x 6.3cm) squares. You will now have two lengths that measure 74½in (189.2cm) long and two lengths that measure 76½in (194.3cm) long.

On to each side of the quilt top sew a 74½in (189.2cm) strip. Press seams outwards.

On to the top and bottom of the quilt top sew a 76½in (194.3cm) strip. Press seams outwards.

8 FINISHING

Sew the two 81in (205.7cm) pieces together to form a piece approximately 81in x 84in (205.7cm x 213.4cm). Layer up the backing, wadding (batting) and quilt top and baste together using your chosen method. Start quilting from the centre and work your way out to the edges.

Join all the binding strips together and press the seams open. Fold the binding strip in half lengthways and press open. Join the binding to the front of the quilt using a ¼in (0.6cm) seam and join the ends. Hand stitch the binding down to the back of the quilt.

A

B

C

CRISS-CROSS PATCHES

SIZE: 55in x 70in
(139.7cm x 177.8cm)

THIS traditional patchwork design is simple yet effective. Choose fabrics with a limited palette of toning colours and offset these against a pale background to create this eyecatching diamond-patterned design.

YOU WILL NEED

○ 2 charm packs (80 squares)

○ 2 charm packs of background fabric (48 squares)

○ 1 yard (0.9m) of background fabric

○ 1¾ yards (1.6m) of fabric for backing

○ ½ yard (0.4m) of fabric for binding

○ Piece of wadding (batting) at least 61in x 76in (154.9cm x 193cm)

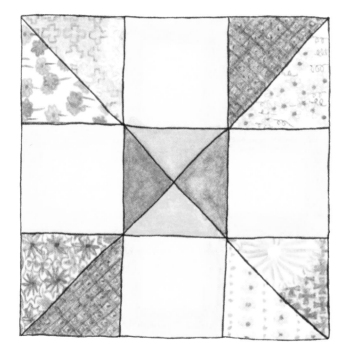

1 PREPARING AND CUTTING FABRICS

From the charm squares choose 60 for the nine-patch blocks and 20 for the small blocks in the sashing.

From the background fabric cut three strips, 14in (35.6cm) x width of fabric. Cross-cut these strips into 30 strips, 4in x 14in (10.2cm x 35.6cm). Then cut one strip, 4in (10.2cm) x width of fabric. From this strip cut one piece, 4in x 14in (10.2cm x 35.6cm).

From the binding fabric cut seven pieces, 63in (160cm) x width of fabric.

2 ASSEMBLING THE NINE-PATCH BLOCKS

For each block take five focus fabric charm squares and four background charm squares. Sew the squares together to form a nine-patch block as per the diagram below. Press the seams outwards to reduce bulk. Complete these steps until you have 12 blocks.

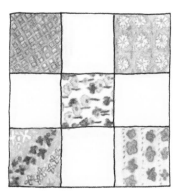

3 CROSS-CUTTING THE BLOCKS

Take two nine-patch blocks and lay one on top of the other. Ensure the seams are lined up and pin together. Take your ruler and draw a line from one corner to the other.

Taking a ¼in (0.6cm) seam, sew a line on both sides of the drawn line. Cut the block diagonally in half down the drawn line. Press seams open. Complete this for all 12 blocks.

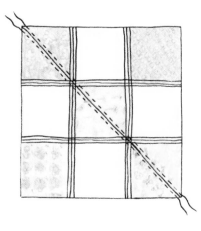

Next, take two of the slashed nine-patch blocks and lay one on top of the other with the diagonal seams on top of each other. Ensure the seams are lined up and pin together. Take your ruler and draw a line from one corner to the other, the opposite corners to the ones that already have the seams. Taking a ¼in (0.6cm) seam, sew a line on both sides of the drawn line. Cut the block diagonally in half down the drawn line. Press seams open. Complete this for all 12 blocks. Trim all blocks to 14in (35.6cm) square.

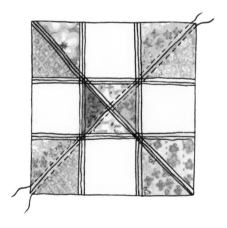

4 PREPARING THE SASHING BLOCKS

From the remaining charm squares, take two and place them on top of each other.

Take your ruler and draw a line from one corner to the other. Taking a ¼in (0.6cm) seam, sew a line on both sides of the drawn line. Cut the squares diagonally in half down the drawn line. Press seams open. Complete this for all remaining charm squares.

Next, take two of the slashed charm squares and lay one on top of the other with the diagonal seam matching. Take your ruler and draw a line from one corner to the other, the opposite corners to the ones that already have the seams. Taking a ¼in (0.6cm) seam, sew a line on both sides of the drawn line. Cut the block diagonally in half down the drawn line. Press seams open. Complete this for all blocks.

Trim these blocks to 4in (10.2cm) square.

5 ASSEMBLING THE TOP

Using the photograph as a guide, lay out the blocks, the sashing blocks and the sashing until you are happy with the placement of the blocks. Sew each strip of blocks together. Press seams open as you go along. Once each row is joined, sew the rows together until the quilt top is complete. Press the seams open as you go along.

6 FINISHING

Layer up the backing, wadding (batting) and quilt top and baste together using your chosen method. Start quilting from the centre and work your way out to the edges.

Join all the binding strips together and press the seams open. Fold the binding strip in half lengthways and press open. Join the binding to the front of the quilt using a ¼in (0.6cm) seam and join the ends. Hand stitch the binding down to the back of the quilt.

TIP
Don't underestimate the impact of a well-chosen binding fabric for your quilt. A contrasting colour works really well for a simple but striking design.

MERRY-GO-ROUND

SIZE: 72in x 90in
(182.9cm x 228.6cm))

THIS gorgeous quilt is made from repeating blocks of spinning circles made from pieced wedges of different-coloured fabric. The resulting geometric design creates a fabulous effect over a whole quilt.

- 1 jelly roll (30 strips)
- ½ yard (0.4m) of fabric for block centres
- 6¼ yards (5.7m) of fabric for background and binding
- 5½ yards (5m) of fabric for backing
- Piece of wadding (batting) at least 78in x 96in (198.1cm x 243.8cm)
- 22 degree wedge ruler
- Glue stick (optional)

1 PREPARING AND CUTTING FABRICS

From the background fabric cut: 13 strips, 10in (25.4cm) wide x width of fabric; nine strips, 6½ in (16.5in) wide x width of fabric; six strips, 2½in (6.3cm) wide x width of fabric; eight strips, 2½in (6.3cm) wide x width of fabric for binding. Remove all selvages.

From the fabric for the block centres cut 20 squares, 5in x 5in (12.7cm x 12.7cm).

From the backing fabric cut two pieces, 96in (243.8cm) long x width of fabric. Remove all selvages.

2 PREPARING THE FOCUS FABRIC WEDGES

Take the 30 focus fabric jelly roll strips and put them together into ten groups of three strips. Sew each group of jelly roll strips together along the width and press all seams. Pressing the seams open prevents the strips distorting too much when pressing and helps keeps them nice and straight.

Following the diagram, lay the wedge ruler on top of the strips so that the bottom of the ruler is at the bottom of the fabric and the 6½in (16.5cm) mark is lined up with the top of the fabric. Cut down both sides.

Then flip the ruler around so that the bottom of the ruler is at the top of the fabric and the 6½in (16.5cm) mark is lined up with the bottom of the fabric. Cut the fabric to create another wedge piece.

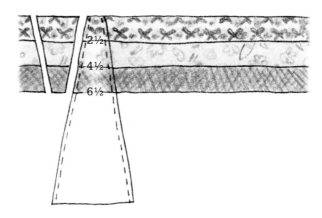

Repeat this until you have 16 wedge pieces per strip. Keep the wedges together in groups of 8, according to the order of the fabrics within the wedge.

Repeat this for all strips so you have 20 groups of wedges in total.

TIP

As you cut the wedges down the length of the fabric, check that the centre of the ruler is square to the edge of the fabric. This will ensure that your wedges are accurate.

3 CUTTING THE BACKGROUND WEDGES

Take the 10in (25.4cm) strips. Lay the wedge ruler on top of the strips so that the bottom of the ruler is at the bottom of the fabric and the 10in (25.4cm) mark is lined up with the top of the fabric. Cut down both sides. Then, as you did with the print fabric wedges, flip the ruler around so that the bottom of the ruler is at the top of the fabric and the 10in (25.4cm) mark is lined up with the bottom of the fabric. Cut another wedge piece. Repeat this until you have 160 wedges. These will be wedge A.

Take the 6½in (16.5cm) strips. Lay the wedge ruler on top of the strips so that the 6in (15.2cm) mark on the ruler is at the bottom of the fabric and the 12½in (31.7cm) mark is lined up with the top of the fabric. Cut down both sides. Again flip the ruler around so that the 6in (15.2cm) mark is at the top of the fabric and the 12½in (31.7cm) mark is lined up with the bottom of the fabric. Cut another wedge piece. Repeat this until you have 80 wedges. These will be wedge B.

Take the 2½in (6.3cm) strips and the leftover fabric from the above strips. Lay the wedge ruler on top of the strips so that the 6in (15.2cm) mark on the ruler is at the bottom of the fabric and the 8½in (21.6cm) mark is lined up with the top of the fabric. Cut down both sides. Again flip the ruler around so that the 6in (15.2cm) mark is at the top of the fabric and the 8½in (21.6cm) mark is lined up with the bottom of the fabric. Cut another wedge piece. Cut the remaining wedges from the leftover fabric from the above wedges until you have 80 wedges. These will be wedge C.

4 ASSEMBLING THE BLOCKS

For each block you will need: one group of eight jelly roll wedges; 8 wedge A; 4 wedge B; 4 wedge C.

Using the diagrams below and overleaf as a guide, sew the wedges together. Sew first into four quarters, then two halves and then sew the whole block together. Press the seams towards the focus fabric.

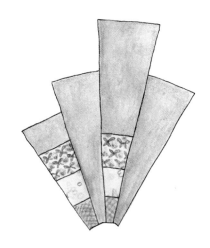

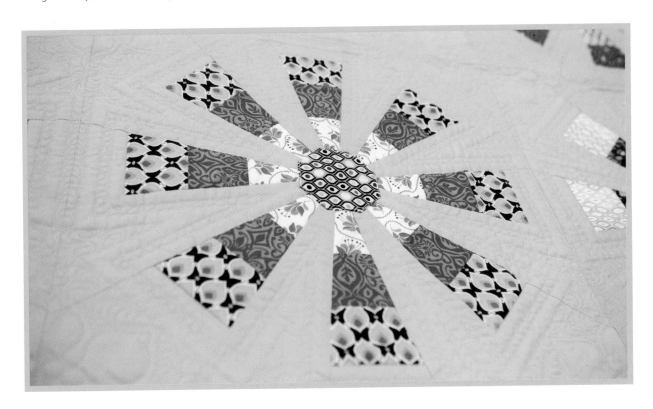

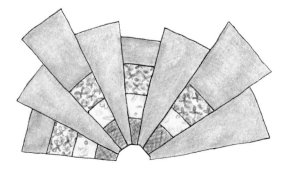

5 PREPARING THE BLOCK CENTRES

Take copies of the octagon paper templates so that you have 20 papers.

Using the English paper piecing method, baste (tack) all the fabric pieces on to the paper templates using a contrasting coloured thread.

Press all centres so that the folds are nice and crisp. A little spray starch helps make the edges really crisp. Clip the basting stitches and then carefully remove the papers.

6 ATTACHING THE CENTRES

Place the octagons in the middle of the block, ensuring that the bottoms of all wedges are under the octagon. Pin them firmly in place. Machine or hand appliqué the octagons in place.

Complete this for all groups of pieces until you have a total of 20 blocks.

Using the centre of the shortest pieces as the horizontal and vertical lines, align these with the lines on your cutting mat and trim each block to 18½in (47cm).

7 ASSEMBLING THE QUILT TOP

Lay out the blocks in four rows of five until you are happy with the placement. Join each strip of blocks together and press the seams. Once each row is joined, sew the rows together until the quilt top is complete. Press the seams as you go along.

TIP

When hand stitching the binding to the back of the quilt, hold the quilt by placing your fingers directly behind where you are sewing to ensure the threads do not go through to the front.

8 PREPARING THE BACKING

Take the two pieces of backing fabric and sew them together so you have a piece measuring approximately 82in x 96in (208.3cm x 243.8cm).

9 FINISHING

Layer up the backing, batting (wadding) and quilt top and baste using your chosen method. Start your quilting from the centre and work your way out to the edges.

Join all the binding strips together and press the seams. Fold the binding strip in half lengthways and press. Join the binding to the front of the quilt using a ¼in (0.6cm) seam. Hand stitch the binding down to the back of the quilt.

TEMPLATE
Shown at 100%

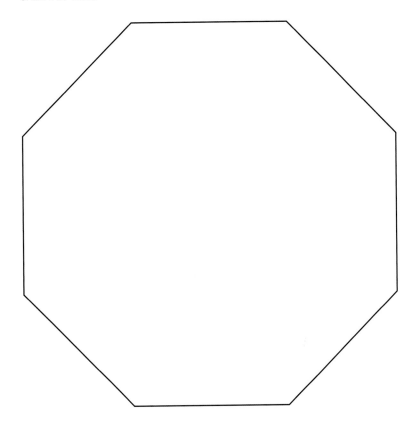

PRETTY PINWHEELS

SIZE: 58in x 72in
(147.3cm x 182.9cm)

THIS deceptively simple patchwork baby quilt is made using machine-pieced blocks and decorated with quilted butterflies and dragonflies. Plain borders and sashing frame and separate the blocks.

YOU WILL NEED

- 1 charm pack (40 squares)*

- 1 jelly roll (27 strips)

- 1 jelly roll of background fabric (17 strips)

- 1 charm pack of background fabric (40 squares)

- 1¾ yards (1.6m) of fabric for backing

- Piece of wadding (batting) at least 64 x 78in (162.6cm x 198.1cm)

*if you want all four pieces of each pinwheel to match either choose a charm pack with two squares of each print, or use two separate charm packs

1 PREPARING AND CUTTING FABRICS

From the charm squares choose 20 sets of two squares for the pinwheels.

From the jelly roll strips choose seven strips for binding. Cut each strip in half and remove all selvages. The remaining 20 strips will be for the pinwheel borders. Cut these jelly roll strips into two strips, 8½in (21.6cm) long, and two strips, 12½in (31.7cm) long.

From the background jelly roll strips cut 15 strips, 12½in (31.7cm) long. Leave the remaining 12 strips uncut.

2 PREPARING THE PINWHEEL BLOCKS

For each pinwheel take two charm squares and two background charm squares.

Make four half-square triangles (see Machine Piecing). Trim each half-square triangle to 4½in (11.4cm) square. Lay the half-square triangles out to form a pinwheel and sew them together taking a ¼in (0.6cm) seam. Press seams open. Trim the pinwheel blocks to 8½in (21.6cm) square.

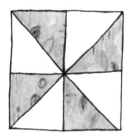

3 FRAMING THE PINWHEELS

To each side of the 20 pinwheel blocks for the front of the quilt, sew a 2½in x 8½in (6.3cm x 21.6cm) strip of jelly roll fabric. Press seams outwards. To each end of the pinwheel blocks sew a 2½in x 12½in (6.3cm x 31.7cm) strip. Press seams outwards. Trim all 20 blocks to 12½in (31.7cm) square.

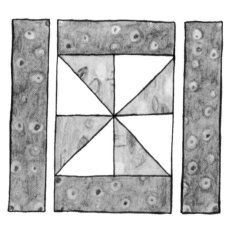

4 PREPARING THE SASHING

Remove the selvages from the remaining 12 background jelly roll strips. Sew them all together end to end, and press seams open.

From the long strip cut four strips, 58½in (148.6cm) long; two strips, 72½in (184.1cm) long; and two strips, 62½in (158.7cm) long.

6 ADDING THE BORDER

Take the two 72½in (184.6cm) strips and sew one strip to each side of the quilt top. Take the two 62½in (158.7cm) strips and sew one strip to the top and one to the bottom of the quilt top. Press seams open as you go along.

7 FINISHING

Layer up the backing fabric, wadding (batting) and quilt top and baste together using your chosen method. Start quilting from the centre and work your way out to the edges.

Join all the four 58½in (148.6cm) strips together and press the seams open. Fold this binding strip in half lengthways and press. Join the binding to the front of the quilt using a ¼in (0.6cm) seam and join the ends. Hand stitch the binding down to the back of the quilt.

5 ADDING THE SASHING AND ASSEMBLING THE ROWS

Lay the blocks out using the quilt photograph as a guide until you are happy with the placement of the blocks. Sew each row of three blocks together, adding a 12½in (31.7cm) strip of background fabric between each one. Press seams towards the blocks.

Once each row is joined, add a sashing between each of the rows and sew the rows together until the quilt top is complete. Press the seams open as you go along.

TIP

When you are joining the rows together, make sure you match the seams of each block as closely as possible and pin the rows well.

TWIRLING WINDMILL

SIZE: 48in x 60in
(121.9cm x 152.4in)

THIS decorative quilt uses fabrics in reds, blues and greens to create a repeating pattern of spinning windmill blocks interspersed with diamond shapes. Pebble quilting completes the effect.

1 PREPARING AND CUTTING FABRICS

From each of the 10 fat eighths cut eight wedge shapes using the template. You will have 80 in total.

From the co-ordinating fat eighths cut 80 pieces, 1¾in x 2¼in (4.4cm x 5.7cm).

From the fabric for the diamonds cut 240 pieces, 2¼in x 3¾in (5.7cm x 9.5cm).

From the binding fabric cut six strips, 2½in (6.3cm) long x width of fabric. Remove all selvages.

From the background fabric cut 160 pieces, 3¼in x 8in (8.2cm x 20.3cm).

From the backing fabric cut: one piece, 54in (137.2cm) x width of fabric; and one piece, 27in (68.6cm) x width of fabric. Cut this second piece in half down the centre to yield two pieces measuring 27in (68.6cm) x width of fabric. Remove all selvages.

2 PREPARING THE FOUNDATION PAPERS

Take 80 copies of the foundation pattern on to printer paper and cut them out roughly.

3 PIECING THE BLOCKS

Take a foundation paper piece and turn it upside down so that the lines are face down. Take one of the wedge shapes cut from the fat eighths and place in the centre of the block, right side up. Hold the paper up to the light and ensure that the edges of the fabric overlap the lines for the centre wedge.

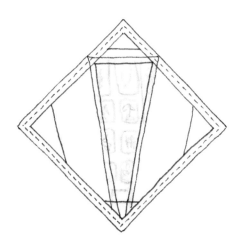

On to one side of the wedge, place a 3¼in x 8in (8.2cm x 20.3cm) strip of background fabric face down, and align the cut edge of the fabric with the cut edge of the wedge. Ensure that the ends of the blocks overlap the edge of the lines on the paper. Hold this up to the light to ensure that the placement of the piece is correct.

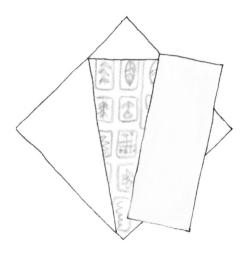

Holding the piece firmly in place, turn the paper over and, with a 1.5mm stitch length, stitch down the line for the side of the wedge.

Fold the paper foundation back and trim the seam allowance to ¼in (0.6cm), flip the background piece back and press gently.

TIP

A dab of glue stick or a pin will keep the first fabric piece in place until it has been stitched down.

Using the same method, add all the remaining pieces in the order shown on the foundation pattern.

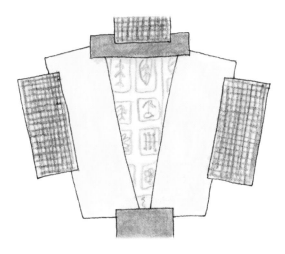

Once the block is complete, trim it using the outside of the foundation paper as a guide and then very gently remove the papers from the back of the block.

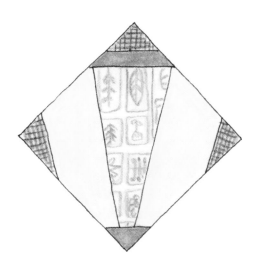

4 ASSEMBLING THE BLOCK

Take four blocks with the same centre wedge fabric and, using the diagram as a guide, sew the blocks together. Trim to 12½in (31.7cm) square. Repeat this for all pieces until you have 20 blocks.

5 ASSEMBLING THE TOP

Lay out the blocks with four across the width and four down the length. Once you are happy with the placement, sew the blocks together into rows, and then sew the rows together. Press the seams as you go along.

6 PREPARING THE BACKING

Take the two pieces of 27in x 42in (68.6cm x 106.7cm) backing fabric and sew them together end to end so you have one piece measuring approximately 54in x 42in (137.2cm x 106.7cm).

Sew the 27in x width of fabric piece down the width of fabric side of the width of fabric x 54in (106.7cm x 137.2cm) piece so that you have a piece measuring approximately 54in x 69in (137.2cm x 175.3cm). Press all seams.

7 FINISHING

Layer up the backing, wadding (batting) and quilt top and baste using your chosen method. Start your quilting from the centre and work your way out to the edges.

Join all the binding strips together and press the seams. Fold the binding strip in half lengthways and press. Join the binding to the front of the quilt using a ¼in (0.6cm) seam. Hand stitch the binding down to the back of the quilt.

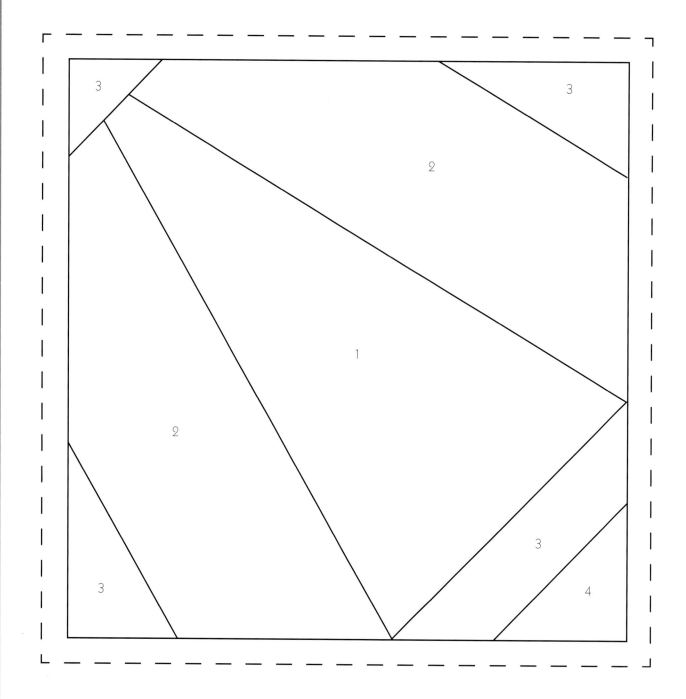

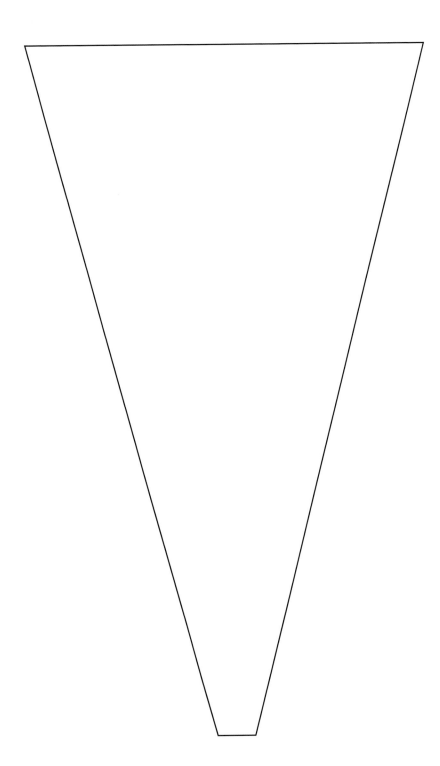

SQUARE ROOT

SIZE: 58in x 76in
(147.3cm x 193cm)

STRIP piecing jelly rolls makes light work of creating this simple colourful quilt. Change the design of the jelly rolls to make this a great quilt for babies and small children or a perfect quilt for snuggling under on cold winter evenings.

- 1 jelly roll of focus fabric for quilt and binding (37 jelly roll strips)

- 1 jelly roll for background (42 jelly roll strips)

- 3½ yards (3.2m) of fabric for backing

- Piece of wadding (batting) at least 65in x 82in (165.1cm x 208.3cm)

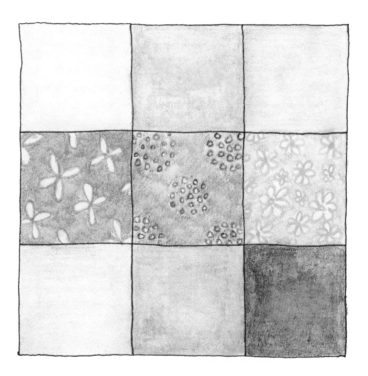

1 PREPARING AND CUTTING FABRICS

From the focus fabric jelly roll strips choose: 30 for the blocks and border; and seven for the binding. Cut the seven binding strips in half and remove the selvages. From one half-strip of binding cut four 2½in (6.3cm) squares and then discard the rest of that half-strip.

From the backing fabric cut two pieces, 63in (160cm) x width of fabric.

2 PREPARING THE STRIPS

Take the 30 focus fabric jelly roll strips and divide them into ten groups of three strips. Sew each group of jelly roll strips together along the length and press all seams.

> **TIP**
>
> Pressing the seams open prevents the strips distorting too much when pressing and helps keeps them nice and straight.

From the ten groups cut a total of 160 strips, 2½in (6.3cm) long.

Take the 42 background jelly roll strips and divide them into 14 groups of three strips. Sew each group of jelly roll strips together along their length and press all seams.

From the 14 groups cut 216 strips, 2½in (6.3cm) long.

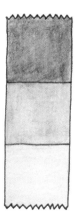

3 ASSEMBLING THE BLOCKS

Take one focus fabric strip. On to each side sew one background strip, matching the seams as closely as possible. Press seams.

Complete this for all strips until you have a total of 108 nine-patch blocks.

4 ASSEMBLING THE QUILT TOP

Lay out the blocks into twelve rows of nine so that the focus fabric runs horizontally across the quilt. Once you are happy with the placement of the blocks, join the blocks together, pressing the seams as you go along.

Once each row is joined, sew the rows together until the quilt top is complete. Press the seams as you go along.

5 ADDING THE BORDER

Sew the remaining focus fabric strips together end to end so that you have two lengths each containing nine units 54½in (138.4cm) long, and two lengths each containing 12 units 72½in (184.1cm) long.

On to each end of both of the 54½in (138.4cm) strips, sew one of the 2½in (6.3cm) squares cut from the half-strip so that they measure 58½in (148.6cm) long.

On to each side of the quilt top sew a 72½in (184.1cm) strip. Press seams outwards. On to the top and bottom of the quilt top sew a 58½in (148.6cm) strip. Press seams outwards.

> ### TIP
>
> When sewing the rows together and when adding the borders, match the seams as closely as possible and pin to hold the pieces together securely during sewing.

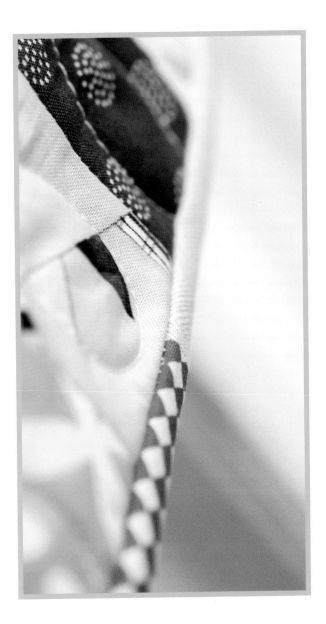

6 FINISHING

Take the two pieces of backing fabric and sew them together so you have a piece measuring approximately 63in x 82in (160cm x 208.3cm).

Layer up the backing, wadding (batting) and quilt top and baste using your chosen method. Start your quilting from the centre and work your way out to the edges.

Join all the binding strips together and press the seams. Fold the binding strip in half lengthways and press. Join the binding to the front of the quilt using a ¼in (0.6cm) seam. Hand stitch the binding down to the back of the quilt.

CONTRAFLOW

SIZE: 76in x 86in
(193cm x 218.4cm)

THIS zigzag quilt is easier to make than it looks as there are no seams to match up. It is simply a matter of piecing the fabric pieces into strips and then joining them together. Follow the pattern carefully and you can't go wrong.

YOU WILL NEED

- 1 layer cake of print fabric (34 squares)
- 1 layer cake of background fabric (37 squares)
- 5 yards (4.6m) of fabric for backing
- ⅔ yard (0.6m) of fabric for binding
- Piece of wadding (batting) at least 82in x 92in (208.3cm x 233.7cm)

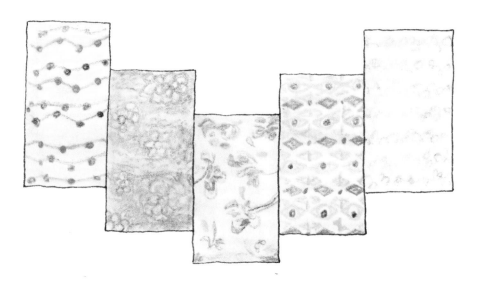

1 PREPARING AND CUTTING FABRICS

Cut the 34 layer cake print fabric squares in half to yield 68 rectangles, 5in x 10in (12.7cm x 25.4cm).

Cut 28 layer cake background fabric squares in half to yield 56 rectangles, 5in x 10in (12.7cm x 25.4cm).

Cut three layer cake background fabric squares in quarters to yield 12 squares, 5in x 5in.

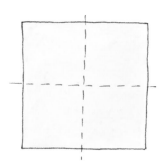

Cut six layer cake background fabric squares in half to yield 12 rectangles, 5in x 10in (12.7cm x 25.4cm). Cross-cut these to yield 12 rectangles, 5in x 7½in (12.7cm x 19cm) and 12 rectangles, 2½in x 5in (6.3cm x 12.7cm).

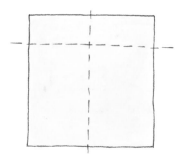

From the backing fabric cut two pieces, 90in (228.6cm) x width of fabric. Remove all selvages.

From the binding fabric cut eight strips, 2½in (6.3cm) x width of fabric. Remove all selvages.

2 ASSEMBLING THE STRIPS

You need 17 strips in total. For each strip take four 5in x 10in (12.7cm x 25.4cm) rectangles of print fabric and three 5in x 10in (12.7cm x 25.4cm) rectangles of background fabric. Starting with a rectangle of print fabric, sew the pieces end to end, alternating between print and background fabric.

Separate the 17 strips into four groups:

Group A – 3 strips

On the top of each strip sew a 5in x 10in (12.7cm x 25.4cm) piece of background fabric, and on the bottom sew a 5in x 2½in (12.7cm x 6.3cm) piece.

Group B – 6 strips

On the top of each strip sew a 5in x 7½in (12.7cm x 19cm) piece of background fabric, and on the bottom sew a 5in (12.7cm) square.

Group C – 6 strips

On the top of each strip sew a 5in (12.7cm) square of background fabric, and on the bottom sew a 5in x 7½in (12.7cm x 19cm) piece.

Group D – 2 strips

On the top of each strip sew a 5in x 2½in (12.7cm x 6.3cm) piece of background fabric, and on the bottom sew a 5in x 10in (12.7cm x 25.4cm) piece.

Press all seams.

4 PREPARING THE BACKING

Take the two pieces of backing fabric and sew them together so you have a piece measuring approximately 82in x 90in (208.3cm x 228.7cm).

5 FINISHING

Layer up the backing, wadding (batting) and quilt top and baste using your chosen method. Start your quilting from the centre and work your way out to the edges.

Join all the binding strips together and press the seams. Fold the binding strip in half lengthways and press. Join the binding to the front of the quilt using a ¼in (0.6cm) seam. Hand stitch the binding down to the back of the quilt.

TIP

Pressing the seams open prevents the strips distorting too much when pressing and helps keeps them nice and straight.

3 ASSEMBLING THE TOP

Lay out the strips according to the diagram below. Once you are happy with the placement, sew the rows together until all strips have been attached. Press the seams as you go along.

C B A B C D C B A B C D C B A B C

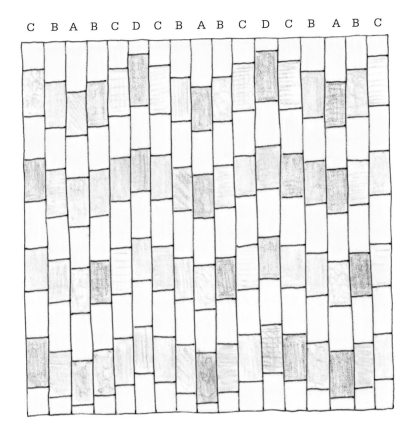

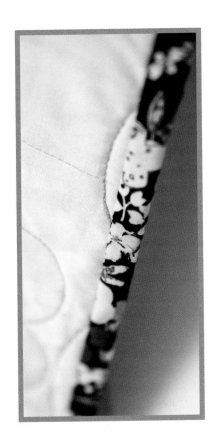

SHURIKEN

SIZE: 72in x 90in
(182.9cm x 228.6cm)

THIS quilt reminds me of fun fairs and merry-go-rounds with its bold primary colours and graphic shapes. This pattern looks way more complicated than it actually is as there are few seams to match, so choose some great fabrics and have fun!

YOU WILL NEED

○ 1 jelly roll (40 strips)

○ 2 layer cakes for background (40 squares in each)

○ 5⅓ yards (4.9m) of fabric for backing

○ ⅔ yard (0.6m) of fabric for binding

○ Piece of wadding (batting) at least 76in x 96in (193.1cm x 243.8cm)

○ Fabric marking pen or pencil suitable for the background colour

1 CUTTING FABRICS

From each of the jelly roll strips, remove the selvages. Then fold each strip in half lengthways. Fold in half again, and then again. Cut along each folded edge with scissors so you have eight equal-sized pieces. The pieces do not have to be 100 per cent accurate so cutting this way will save time.

From the 80 background layer cakes cut 320 squares, 5in x 5in (12.7cm x 12.7cm).

From the binding fabric cut eight pieces, 2½in (6.3cm) x width of fabric. Remove all selvages.

From the backing fabric cut two pieces, 96in (243.8cm) x width of fabric. Remove all selvages.

2 PREPARING THE BACKGROUND PIECES

Take one 5in (12.7cm) square cut from the background layer cake fabric and lay it on your cutting board so the edges are aligned with the lines on your cutting mat.

Using a ruler and a fabric marking pen or pencil, draw a line between the 2in (5.1cm) mark on the left edge of the piece to the 4½in (11.4cm) mark on the bottom of the piece as in the diagram. Repeat this for all squares.

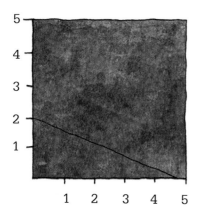

TIP

For light background colours, you could use an air-removable pen, a water-soluble pen or a pencil to mark your lines. For darker background colours, use tailor's chalk or pale coloured fabric-marking pencils.

3 MAKING THE BLOCKS

For each block take four 5in (12.7cm) squares of background layer cake fabric. On each of the drawn lines lay a strip cut from the jelly roll strips, making sure that the zigzag edge of the strip is lined up with the drawn line.

Attach the strip to the background fabric by sewing a seam ⅛in (0.3cm) from the edge of the strip. Repeat this for all four pieces.

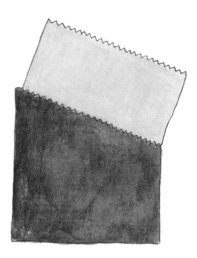

Trim off the excess background fabric and then trim the block to 5in (12.7cm) square.

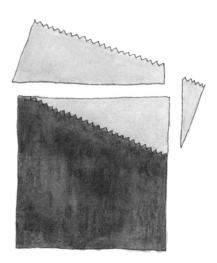

4 ASSEMBLING THE QUILT TOP

Join each strip of blocks together and press the seams. Once each row is joined, sew the rows together until the quilt top is complete. Press the seams as you go along.

5 PREPARING THE BACKING

Sew the two pieces of backing fabric together so you have a piece measuring approximately 82in x 96in (208.3cm x 243.8cm).

6 FINISHING

Layer the backing, wadding (batting) and quilt top and baste using your chosen method.

Start quilting from the centre and work your way out to the edges.

Join all the binding strips together and press the seams. Fold the binding strip in half lengthways and press.

Join the binding to the front of the quilt using a ¼in (0.6cm) seam and join the ends. Hand stitch the binding down to the back of the quilt.

Sew the four squares together as shown in the diagram below. Press seams as you go along.

Repeat this until you have 80 blocks. Trim all blocks to 9½in x 9½in (24.1cm x 24.1cm) square.

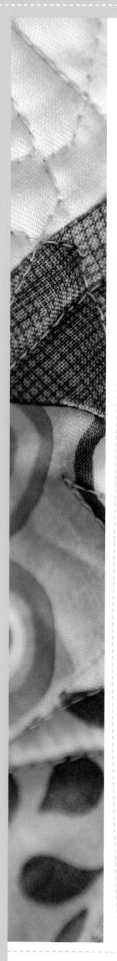

STARS AND STRIPES

SIZE: 60in x 80in
(152.4cm x 20.3cm)

THIS fabulous quilt incorporates stars, squares, diamonds and stripes in a colourful geometric kaleidoscope. It uses a combination of strip-pieced jelly rolls and pre-cut charm squares and is finished with quilted star patterns.

- 1 jelly roll (39 strips)

- 1 charm pack (40 squares)

- 1¾ yards (1.6m) of fabric for stars

- 1¾ yards (1.6m) of background fabric

- 4 yards (3.6m) of fabric for backing

- Piece of wadding (batting) at least 66in x 86in (167.6cm x 218.4cm)

- Template plastic or piece of card at least 4¼in (10.8cm) square

- Marking pen or pencil

1 PREPARING AND CUTTING FABRICS

From the jelly roll strips choose 32 strips for the pieced sections and seven strips for the binding. Remove the selvages and cut the seven binding strips in half.

From the fabric for stars cut 48 squares, 5in (12.7cm). Cut these diagonally to yield 96 triangles. From the same fabric, cut 48 strips, 2¼in x 5in (5.7cm x 12.7cm), and 48 strips, 2¼in x 8½in (5.7cm x 21.6cm).

From the background fabric cut 48 strips, 2½in x 8½in (6.3cm x 21.6cm) and 48 strips, ½in x 12½in (6.3cm x 31.7cm).

From the backing fabric cut two pieces, 42in x 72in (106.7cm x 182.9cm). Remove all selvages.

2 PREPARING THE STRIPY UNITS

Take 32 jelly roll strips for the pieced sections and put them together into eight groups of four strips. Sew each group of jelly roll strips together along the width and press all seams open. Pressing the seams open prevents the strips distorting too much and helps keep them nice and straight. From each of the eight groups cut three 12½in (31.7cm) units.

3 ADDING THE STAR POINTS

On a piece of template plastic or card, draw a 4⅛in (10.5cm) square. Draw a line diagonally across the square, and cut out one of the triangles. This is the template that will be used to help you place the star points correctly. On each of the four corners of each long stripy unit, place the template in the corner and draw a line from one edge of the fabric to the other (see the diagram).

On each of the drawn lines lay a triangle cut from the 5in (12.7cm) squares, making sure that the edge of the triangle is lined up with the drawn line and that the outer points overlap the edges of the unit by the same amount at each side (see the diagram).

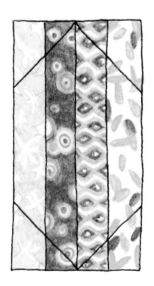

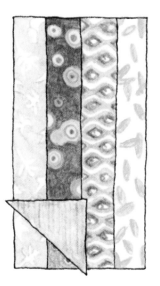

Using a ¼in (0.6cm) seam allowance down the edge of the triangle, attach the triangle to the stripy unit. Complete all of the corners in the same way. Trim the excess fabric from the back, fold back the triangles and press.

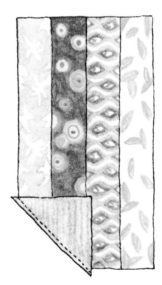

Trim the excess fabric away so that the long units measure 12½in x 8½in (31.7cm x 21.6cm). Take seven blocks and cut them in half across the width so that you have 14 blocks measuring 6¼in x 8½in (15.9cm x 21.6cm).

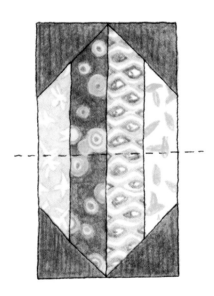

4 PREPARING THE STAR CENTRE BLOCKS

Take 24 charm squares and to two sides of each one sew a 2¼in x 5in (5.7cm x 12.7cm) strip of star fabric. Press seams outwards. To each end then sew a 2¼in x 8½in (5.7cm x 21.6cm) strip of star fabric.

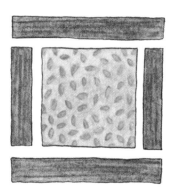

Press seams outwards. To each side of each block sew a 2¼in x 8½in (5.7cm x 21.6cm) strip of star fabric. Press seams outwards. To each end then sew a 2¼in x 12½in (5.7cm x 31.7cm) strip of star fabric. Press seams outwards. Trim all blocks to 8½in (21.6cm) square.

5 PREPARING THE SPACER BLOCKS

Take 12 of the star centre blocks. To each side of the block sew a 2¼in x 8½in (5.7cm x 21.6cm) strip of background fabric. Press seams outwards. To the top and bottom of each block sew a 2¼in x 12½in strip of background fabric. Press seams outwards.

Trim all 12 blocks to 12½in (31.7cm) square. Take five of the blocks and cut them in half across so that you have ten half-blocks that measure 6¼in x 12¼in (15.9cm x 31.1cm).

Take one block and cut it in half across, and then in half again so that you have four quarter blocks that measure 6¼in (15.9cm) square.

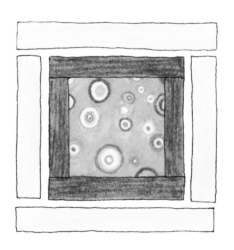

TIP

Use a little spray starch on your blocks before trimming them. This helps to make all the seams nice and flat, which helps with accuracy when trimming the blocks to size. It also adds stability to the blocks and prevents them from stretching when you sew them together.

6 ASSEMBLING THE TOP

Lay the blocks out using the diagram as a guide until you are happy with the placement of the blocks. Sew each row of blocks together, taking a ¼in (0.6cm) seam. Press seams open. Then sew the rows together until the quilt top is complete. Press the seams open as you go along.

7 ASSEMBLING THE BACKING

Sew the remaining 16 charm squares so that they form a row measuring 5in x 72½in (12.7 x 184.1cm). Sew the row of charm squares to one side of the 72in (182.9cm) length of backing fabric and then sew the last piece of backing fabric on to the other side. Press seams open. You will now have a piece that measures approximately 72in x 88in (182.9cm x 223.5cm).

8 FINISHING

Layer up the backing, wadding (batting) and quilt top and baste together using your chosen method. Start quilting from the centre and work your way out to the edges. Join all the binding strips together and press the seams open. Fold the binding strip in half lengthways and press. Join the binding to the front of the quilt using a ¼in (0.6cm) seam and join the ends. Hand stitch the binding down to the back of the quilt.

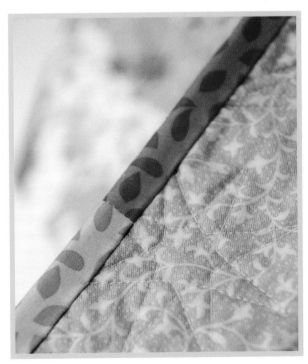

GIANT'S CAUSEWAY

SIZE: 86in x 86in
(218.4cm x 218.4cm)

THIS complicated looking quilt is easier than it looks. As long as you cut out the paper pieces accurately, the pattern is easily accomplished. Be bold with your colour choice of fabrics for a stunning design.

YOU WILL NEED

- 16 fat quarters of focus fabric

- 3 yards (2.8m) of background fabric A for centres, long diamonds and large octagons

- 2¾ yards (2.5m) of background fabric B for squares for main background

- 5¾ yards (5.2m) of fabric for backing

- ⅔ yard (0.7m) of fabric for binding

- Piece of wadding at least 92in x 92in (233.7cm x 233.7cm)

- Template plastic

- Marker pen

- Printer paper

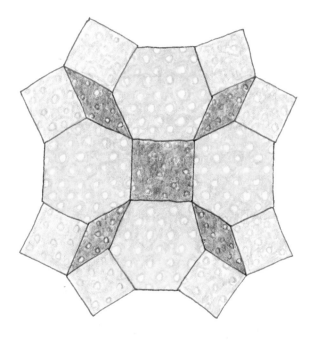

1 PREPARING AND CUTTING FABRICS

From each fat quarter cut four pieces, 4½in x 22in (11.4cm x 55.9cm). Cross-cut these at 5in (12.7cm) so that you have 16 pieces from each fat quarter.

From background fabric A cut: 64 pieces, 2½in (6.3cm) square; 256 shapes of template A; 49 pieces, 5½in (14cm) square; 28 rectangles, 3in x 6in (7.6cm x 15.2cm); and four pieces, 3in (7.6cm) square.

From background fabric B cut: 504 pieces, 2½in (6.3cm) square; and 112 strips, 2½in x 6in (6.3cm x 15.2cm).

From the binding fabric cut eight pieces, 2½in (6.3cm) x width of fabric.

From the backing fabric cut: two pieces, 92in (233.7cm) x width of fabric; and three pieces, 7in (17.8cm) x width of fabric. Remove all selvages.

2 PREPARING THE TEMPLATES

Trace template C and D on to template plastic using permanent marker. Carefully cut out.

3 PREPARING THE PAPER PIECES

You will need the following number of paper shapes: 256 hexagons (template B); 576 squares (template A); and 112 strips with triangle ends (template D). Photocopy each template and repeat several times to create a sheet of each shape. Then photocopy each sheet until you have the required number of paper shapes.

Cut these paper pieces out by stapling several sheets of shapes together and cutting along the lines on the top sheet.

4 ENGLISH PAPER PIECING

Tack (baste) all the fabric pieces on to paper templates using a contrasting thread (see English Paper Piecing).

5 CONSTRUCTING BLOCKS

You will need 64 blocks in total and for each block you will need: four hexagons of focus fabric of one design; one flower centre of background fabric B; eight squares of background fabric A; and four long diamonds of background fabric B.

Arrange and hand sew the pieces together as per the diagrams, ensuring that the edges of the pieces are lined up as accurately as possible (see English Paper Piecing).

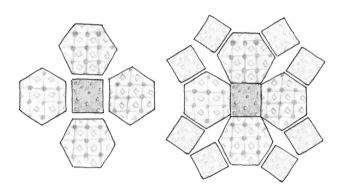

Once the pieces have been joined together, add the long thin triangles. Firstly sew the corners of the background squares together as per the diagram. Turn the block over, place the triangles over the spaces and pin securely.

Stitch the edges of the background pieces down to the diamonds in the same way you would for appliqué. If you wish, you could use water-based glue stick or appliqué glue to hold the diamond and large polygon appliqué pieces in place while you do this.

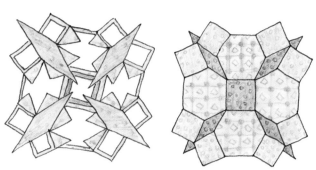

6 CONSTRUCTING THE ROWS

Sew the blocks into eight rows of eight blocks, inserting triangle strip pieces between the blocks. Do not add triangle strip pieces to the end of each row.

7 ASSEMBLING THE TOP

Lay the rows out and sew together, inserting triangle strip pieces between the rows. You will have holes where the octagons should be – these will be added in next.

To fill in the half-octagons around the edges of the quilt, again tuck the ends of the diamonds in and place the 3in x 6in (7.6cm x 15.2cm) rectangles over the half-octagon shapes and pin securely. Again stitch the edges of the English paper pieces down to the octagons.

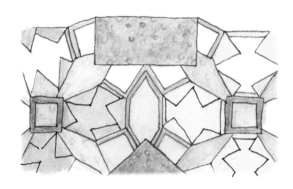

8 ADDING THE OCTAGONS

Once the rows have been joined, turn the quilt top over, tuck the ends of the diamonds in and place the 5½in (14cm) squares of background fabric A over the octagon shapes and pin securely.

You could use water-based glue stick or appliqué glue to firmly adhere the pieces in place. Stitch the edges of the English paper pieces down to the octagons.

9 TRIMMING THE QUILT TOP

Line your ruler up with the edge of the hexagons and draw a line. Sew around the quilt top ⅛in (0.3cm) from the drawn line and edge of the hexagons using a short stitch length. Trim the quilt along the drawn lines.

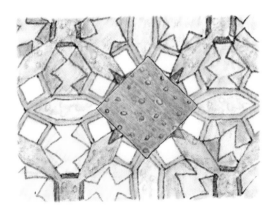

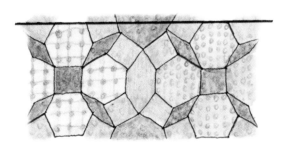

10 REMOVING THE PAPERS

Snip all the threads on the face of the quilt top and gently ease all the papers out. If you use the English paper piecing method described in the Materials and Techniques section, you do not need to remove the threads as when you will the papers out the threads will automatically be pulled through to the back.

11 FINISHING

Sew the backing pieces together down their length to give you a piece that measures 86in x 92in (218.4cm x 233.7cm).

Sew the three 7in (17.8cm) strips end to end and trim to 92in (233.7cm) long. Sew this piece down the length of the backing so that you have a piece that measures approximately 90in x 92in (228.6cm x 233.7cm). Press seams.

Layer up the backing, wadding (batting) and quilt top and baste using your chosen method.

Join all the binding strips together and press the seams. Join the binding to the front of the quilt and join the ends. Hand stitch the binding down to the back of the quilt.

PAPER PIECES AND TEMPLATES
Shown at 100%

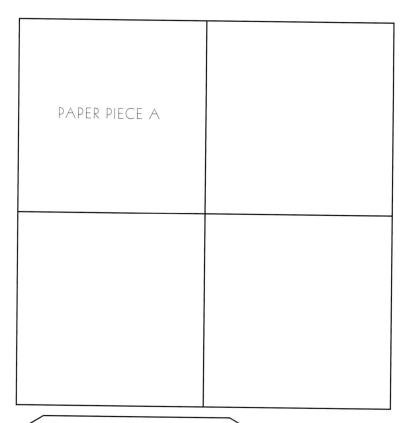

PAPER PIECE A

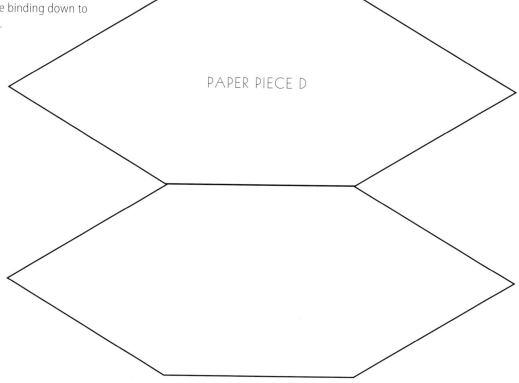

PAPER PIECE D

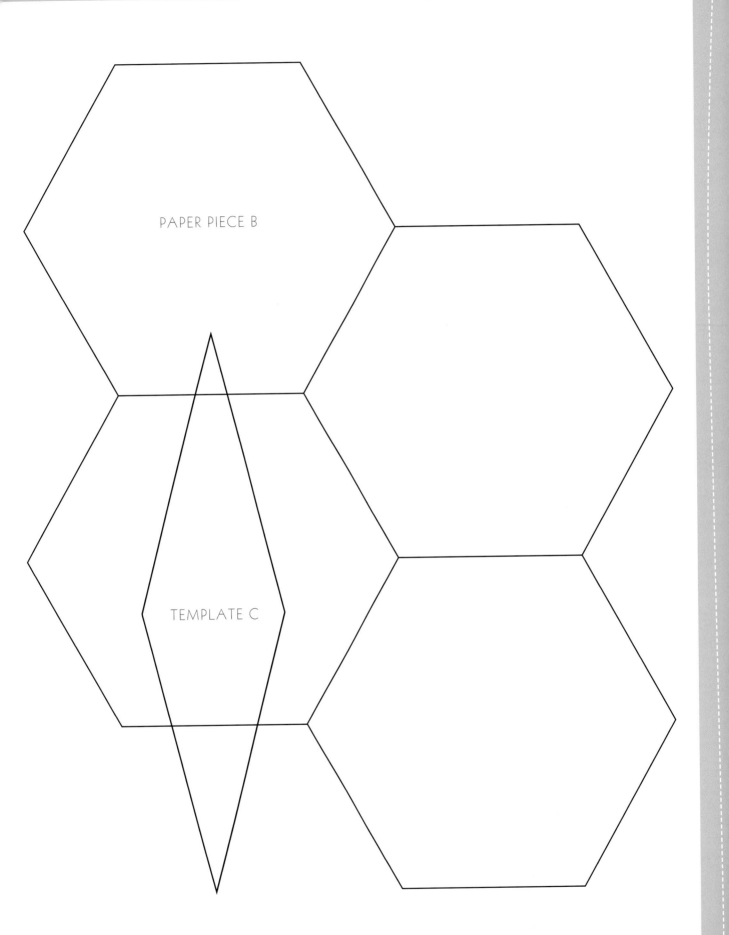

PAPER PIECE B

TEMPLATE C

EASY PEASY PLACE MATS

SIZE: 14½in
(36.8cm) square

THESE graphic place mats will brighten up any table. Made using brightly coloured jelly roll strips, cut and pieced together, they are simplicity itself.

FOR A SET OF 4 PLACEMATS:

YOU WILL NEED

- 12 jelly roll strips
- ½ yard (0.4m) of background fabric
- 1 yard (0.9m) of fabric for backing
- 4 pieces of wadding (batting) 18in (45.7cm) square
- Spray starch (optional)

1 PREPARING AND CUTTING FABRICS

From the jelly roll strips choose: six for the placemats; and six for the binding. Remove the selvages and cut all strips in half.

From the background fabric cut: four squares, 6½in (16.5cm); one strip, 6½in x 22in (16.5cm x 55.9cm); two strips, 2½in x 22in (6.3cm x 55.9cm); and eight strips, 2½in x 6½in (6.3cm x 16.5cm).

From the backing fabric cut four squares, 18in (45.7cm).

2 ASSEMBLING THE UNITS

Unit A
Take seven half jelly roll strips and lay them out side by side until you are happy with the order. Sew the strips together to form one piece measuring 14½in x approximately 22in (36.8cm x approximately 55.9cm).

Unit C

Square the edge and then cut each piece down the length so that you have eight strips, 2½in x 14½in (6.3cm x 36.8cm).

4 ASSEMBLING THE PLACE MATS

For each place mat you will need two strips from each of unit A, B and C. You will also need one 6½in (16.5cm) square and two 2½in x 6½in (6.3cm x 16.5cm) strips of background fabric.

Using the diagram as a guide, lay out all the pieces for the four place mats until you are happy with the placement. Sew the units together, pressing seams as you go.

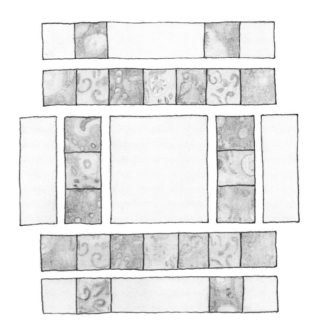

Unit B

Take three half jelly roll strips and lay them out side by side until you are happy with the order. Sew the strips together to form one piece measuring 6½in x approximately 22in (16.5cm x approximately 55.9cm).

Unit C

Take the 6½in x 22in (16.5cm x 55.9cm) strip of background fabric and the two remaining half jelly roll strips and sew one to the bottom and one to the top of the background piece.

Take the two 2½in x 22in (6.3cm x 55.9cm) background fabric strips and sew one to the bottom and one to the top of the background piece. The piece should measure 14½in x 22in (36.8cm x 55.9cm).

Press all seams open to reduce bulk. Some spray starch may be useful at this point to get the piece to lay flat.

3 CUTTING THE UNITS

Unit A

Square the edge and then cut each piece down the length so that you have eight strips, each measuring 2½in x 14½in (6.3cm x 36.8cm).

Unit B

Square the edge and then cut each piece down the length so that you have eight strips, 2½in x 6½in (6.3cm x 16.5cm).

5 FINISHING

Layer up the backing, wadding (batting) and place mat and baste using your chosen method.

Join the binding strips into four groups of two and press in half lengthways. Join one binding strip to the front of each place mat and hand stitch the binding to the back.

WINTERBERRY TABLE RUNNER

SIZE: 14in x 70in
(35.6cm x 177.8cm)

THIS is the perfect winter table runner, ideal for Christmas and other holiday celebrations, but simple and cheerful enough to adorn your dining table throughout those long, cold months of autumn and winter.

YOU WILL NEED

- 4 fat eighths of focus fabric in colour A
- 3 fat eighths of focus fabric in colour B
- ¾ yard (0.7m) of background fabric
- 1 yard (0.9m) of backing fabric
- Piece of binding fabric, 10in (25.4cm) x width of fabric
- Piece of cotton wadding (batting) at least 18in x 74in (45.7cm x 188cm)
- Fabric marking pencil
- ¾ yard (0.7m) of fusible web

1 PREPARING AND CUTTING FABRICS

Take three fat eighths of colour A and two of colour B and from each cut two squares, 9in x 9in (22.9cm x 22.9cm).

Take the remaining fat eighth of colour A and cut eight strips, 1¾in x 9in (4.4cm x 22.9cm).

Take the remaining fat eighth of colour B and cut 12 strips, 1¾in x 9in (4.4cm x 22.9cm).

From the background fabric cut 20 squares, 9in x 9in (22.9cm x 22.9cm), together with 20 strips, 1¾in x 9in (4.4cm x 22.9cm).

From the backing fabric cut two strips, 18in (45.7cm) x width of fabric. Remove the selvages.

From the binding fabric cut four strips, 2½in (6.3cm) x width of fabric.

2 MAKING THE HALF-SQUARE TRIANGLES

Take a 9in (22.9cm) square of background fabric and lay a 9in (22.9cm) square of print fabric on top of it so that the edges are aligned.

Take your ruler and draw a line with a fabric marking pencil from one corner to the other. Using a ¼in (0.6cm) seam, sew a line in from both sides of the drawn line. Cut the square diagonally in half down the drawn line. Press the seams open. Complete this for all ten squares.

3 CROSS-CUTTING THE HALF-SQUARE TRIANGLES

Take two of the half-square triangle units and lay one on top of the other with both diagonal seams facing the same way, but ensure that the coloured side of the top piece is placed over the background side of the bottom one and vice versa.

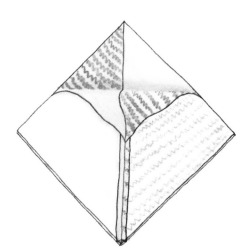

Ensure that the seams are lined up as accurately as possible and pin together. Take your ruler and draw a line from one corner to the other, but the opposite corners to the ones that already have the seams.

Using a ¼in (0.6cm) seam, sew a line in from both sides of the drawn line. Cut the block diagonally in half down the drawn line. Press the seams open. Complete this for all blocks.

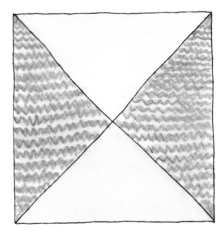

4 CONSTRUCTING THE BLOCKS

Using the diagram as a guide, lay out the small blocks. Sew the four blocks together to make one larger block. Complete these for all of the squares so that you have five blocks in total. Trim the blocks to 14½in x 14½in (36.8cm x 36.8cm) square.

5 PREPARING THE HOLLY LEAVES

Take one each of the 1¾in (4.4cm) strips and sew them together. Press the seams open to avoid the strip distorting and to reduce bulk.

Cut each strip in half across the width. Turn round one of the pieces and sew it back on to the end, ensuring that the centre seams are aligned.

You must ensure that the placement of the two fabrics is exactly as shown in the diagram, as when the holly leaves are added to the blocks the focus fabric needs to be placed where the background fabric is on the blocks.

Place the holly template on to the fusible web and draw around it. You will need 20 holly shapes. Cut them out roughly.

On to the back of each strip, place a fusible web holly leaf and align the points of the leaves exactly on each seam. Press following the manufacturer's instructions to adhere the leaves to the blocks. Cut out accurately along the drawn lines.

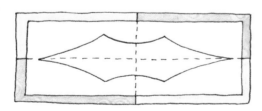

6 ADDING THE HOLLY LEAVES TO THE BLOCKS

Take a block of fabric A and four leaves of fabric B. Place the holly leaves on to the blocks following the diagram, making sure that all the seams are aligned with the blocks' seams. Once you are happy with the placement, press the blocks following the manufacturer's instructions to adhere the leaves to the blocks.

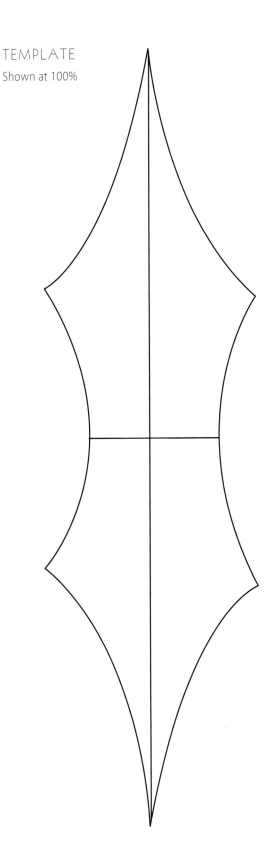

7 ASSEMBLING THE TOP

Lay the five blocks out in a row, alternating the two colours until you are happy with the placement. Sew the row of blocks together and press the seams open.

8 PREPARING THE BACKING

Sew the two back pieces together end to end so that you have a piece measuring approximately 18in x 84in (45.7cm x 213.4cm).

9 LAYERING AND QUILTING

Layer the backing, wadding (batting) and table runner and baste using your chosen method.

Start quilting from the centre and work your way out to the edges. As you reach the holly leaves, stitch around them approximately ⅛in (0.6cm) from the edge of each holly leaf to fix them permanently to the table runner.

10 BINDING

Join all the binding strips together and press the seams open. Fold the binding strip in half lengthways and press.

Join the binding to the front of the table runner using a ¼in (0.6cm) seam and join the ends. Hand stitch the binding down to the back.

DASHER BATHMAT

SIZE: 24in x 36in
(61cm x 91.4cm)

THIS graphic patterned bathmat uses vividly coloured fabric in a simple yet traditional churn dash design to great effect. Backing the mat with a bath towel ensures this project will have a practical as well as aesthetic application.

YOU WILL NEED

- 9 layer cake squares of focus fabric
- 11 layer cake squares for background
- 1 fat eighth for block centres (if you are fussy cutting the centres you may need more to yield 9 motifs, see Techniques)
- 1 bath towel
- 1 piece of cotton wadding (batting) at least 28in x 40in (71.1cm x 101.6cm)
- Perle cotton or embroidery floss for hand quilting
- 1 fat quarter for binding

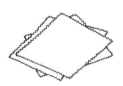

1 PREPARING AND CUTTING FABRICS

From each of the nine focus fabric and nine background fabric pieces cut two squares, 5in x 5in (12.7cm x 12.7cm); and four strips, 2½in x 10in (6.3cm x 25.4cm).

From the background fabric squares cut 12 strips, 1in x 10in (2.5cm x 25.4cm); cross-cut these strips to yield 12 strips, 1in x 3½in (2.5cm x 8.9cm) and 12 strips, 1in x 4½in (2.5cm x 11.4cm).

From the centre fabric cut nine squares, 4½in x 4½in (11.4cm x 11.4cm).

From the bath towel cut one square, 24½in x 24½in (62.2cm x 62.2cm).

From the binding fabric cut seven strips, 2½in x 22in (6.3cm x 55.9cm).

2 ASSEMBLING THE BLOCKS

To each side of the six centre squares, sew a 1in x 3½in (2.5cm x 8.9cm) strip of background fabric. Press seams outwards. To each end of the centre squares, sew a 1in x 4½in (2.5cm x 11.4cm) strip of background fabric. Press seams outwards and if necessary trim to 4½in (11.4cm).

For each block take two 5in (12.7cm) squares of focus and two 5in (12.7cm) squares of background fabric. Lay them on top of each other; draw a line from one corner to the other.

Using a ¼in (0.6cm) seam, sew a line in from both sides of the drawn line. Cut the square diagonally in half down the drawn line. Press the seams open. Complete this for all ten squares and trim each one to 4½in (11.4cm) square.

Take the two 2½in x 10in (6.3cm x 25.4cm) strips of focus fabric and sew each one to a 2½in x 10in (6.3cm x 25.4cm) strip of background fabric. Press the seams and then cut each strip into two 4½in (11.4cm) squares.

Using the diagram below, sew the half-square triangles, strips and centres together to form a churn dash block. Press seams as you go along. Repeat for all the blocks and trim the blocks to 12½in (31.7cm) square.

3 ASSEMBLING THE TOP

Lay the six blocks out in two rows of three until you are happy with the placement.

Sew each row of blocks together and press the seams. Sew the rows together until the bath mat top is complete. Press the seams as you go along.

4 FINISHING

Layer the bath towel, cotton wadding (batting) and bathmat top and baste using your chosen method.

Lightly quilt the bathmat through all the layers to secure the towel backing to the top.

Join all the binding strips together and press the seams. Fold the binding strip in half lengthways and press. Join the binding to the front of the bathmat using a ¼in (0.6cm) seam and join the ends. Hand stitch the binding down to the back of the bath mat.

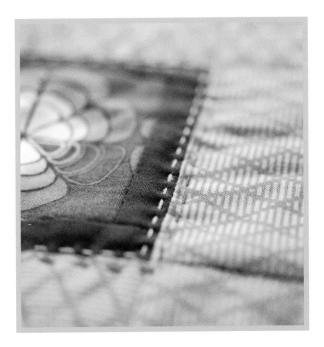

TIP

To make the hand quilting a little easier when quilting through both the top and the towel backing, choose areas to hand quilt that have the least seams.

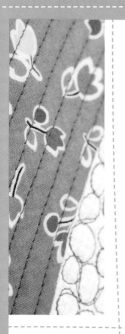

BIG AND BOLD CIRCLES CUSHION

SIZE: 29½in
(74.9cm) square

CREATE a wow factor in your living room with this fabulous cushion. The different shapes of the patches are echoed within the design by repeating lines and circles of quilting on the background fabric, creating an eyecatching effect.

YOU WILL NEED

- 8 layer cake pieces of print fabric

- 1 yard (0.9m) of fabric for cushion back

- 8 layer cake pieces of background fabric

- 2 yards (1.8m) of muslin (or similar) for cushion lining

- 1 fat quarter for binding

- Piece of wadding (batting) at least 32in x 32in (81.3cm x 81.3cm)

- ¼ yard (0.2m) of co-ordinating thin or cord elastic

- Template plastic or cardboard

- Jenny Pedigo curved ruler (optional)

- 30in (76.2cm) cushion pad

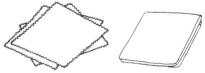

1 CUTTING FABRICS

From the layer cake pieces of both the print fabric and background fabric cut all 16 pieces in half diagonally.

From the cushion lining fabric cut one 34in (86.4cm) square; and two pieces, 16in x 29½in (40.6cm x 74.9cm).

From the cushion back fabric cut one 29½in (74.9cm) square; and two pieces, 16in x 29½in (40.6cm x 74.9cm).

From the elastic cut three 3in (7.6cm) pieces.

From the binding fabric cut six strips, 2½in x 22in (6.3cm x 55.9cm).

2 MAKING THE CUSHION

Follow the instructions for the Circles Squared quilt to cut the curved pieces and make the basic blocks.

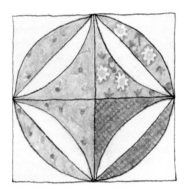

3 ASSEMBLING THE CUSHION TOP

Lay out the completed blocks using the photo of the cushion as a guide. Once you are happy with the placement, sew each row together and press seams. Then sew the rows together. Press seams. Layer up the backing, wadding (batting) and cushion top. Quilt as for the Circles Squared quilt. Trim the quilted cushion top to 29½in (74.9cm) square.

4 PREPARING THE CUSHION BACK

To add the elastic buttonholes, take one cushion back piece and the elastic pieces. Fold each in half and place the first one in the centre of the top, and the second and third pieces halfway between the centre and the edge. Pin in place. Backstitch the elastic ⅛in (0.3cm) from the edge to secure.

Place each of the two cushion back pieces right side up and lay a lining piece on top, aligning the long edges. Sew a seam down the long edge of each piece.

Turn each piece so that the right sides are facing outwards, and press. Topstitch down the long edge.

5 MAKING UP THE CUSHION

Lay the cushion front face down. Lay each of the back pieces right side out, so that the raw edges are aligned with the cushion edge and the topstitched edges overlap in the centre of the cushion. Ensure that the piece with the elastic loops is on the top. Pin firmly in place.

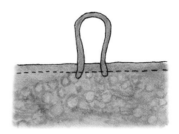

Sew around the edge of the cushion to secure all the layers. Remove all pins. Bind the edges following the instructions for the Circles Squared quilt.

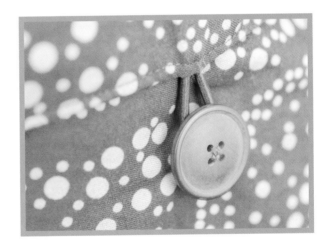

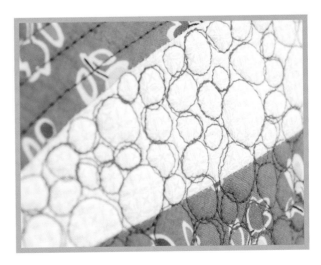

JAUNTY BUTTON-DOWN IPAD CASE

SIZE: 8¼in x 9¾in
(20.9cm x 24.8cm)

THIS delightful iPad case is made using machine-pieced fabric blocks stitched in rows to form a decorative diamond pattern. Choose fabric colours to co-ordinate with your wardrobe for a truly individual style.

YOU WILL NEED

- 7 charm squares
- 1 fat quarter of muslin or scrap fabric
- 1 fat quarter for back and lining
- 2 pieces of wadding (batting) at least 11in x 13in (28cm x 33cm)
- 3in (7.6cm) of narrow elastic
- Button

1 PREPARING AND CUTTING FABRICS

From each of the charm squares cut four squares, 2½in x 2½in (6.3cm x 6.3cm).

From the muslin fabric cut two pieces, 11in x 13in (28cm x 33cm).

From the back and lining fabric cut three pieces, 8¾in x 10½in (22.2cm x 26.7cm).

2 MAKING THE FRONT

Using the diagram as a guide, lay out the small squares in rows until you are happy with the placement.

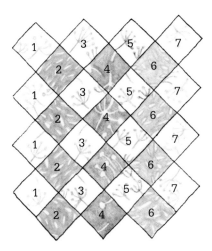

Taking a ¼in (0.6cm) seam, join each row of blocks together and press the seams open. Sew the rows together, ensuring that the seams of each row are lined up with each other. Press the seams towards the outside of the piece.

3 QUILTING

Layer up the muslin, wadding (batting) and iPad front top and quilt as desired. Trim the front to 8½in x 10½in (21.6cm x 26.7cm) using the diagram below as a guide.

Repeat this for the back and trim to 8¾in x 10½in (22.2cm x 26.7cm).

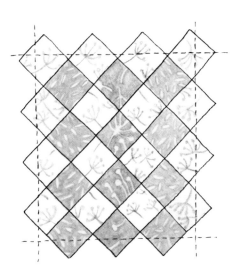

4 ASSEMBLY

Fold the length of elastic in half and place it in the centre of the right side of the case front, so that the raw edges of the elastic are lined up with the raw edges of the front piece. Pin the elastic in place and backstitch over the ends ⅛in (0.3cm) from the edge to secure. Place the front and back pieces right sides together so that the elastic is at the top. Sew both sides and the bottom together with a ¼in (0.6cm) seam. Turn right sides out.

Place both the lining pieces right sides together and sew together along the two sides and bottom, leaving a 3in (7.6cm) gap at the bottom. Put the iPad cover inside the lining so that the two right sides are facing each other. Pin so that the side seams of each piece match each other. Sew all the way around the top ¼in (0.6cm) from the edge.

5 FINISHING

Turn the whole thing right side out through the hole in the bottom of the lining. Flatten the top seam. Pin through all layers and topstitch ⅛in (0.3cm) down from the top of the bag. Tuck the raw edges inside and sew the bottom seam of the lining closed. Sew the button securely in the centre of the middle square at the top of the case.

STARBURST TOTE BAG

SIZE: 14½in x 14½in x 4in
(36.8cm x 36.8cm x 10.2cm)
with a 43in (109.2cm) strap

HAVE fun making this cheerful starburst bag in a multitude of bright colours. The hardest part is folding the triangles accurately, but once you've mastered this, it's a case of colours by numbers!

YOU WILL NEED

- 16 jelly roll strips
- 1 fat quarter of muslin
- ½ yard (0.4m) of home decor weight fabric
- ½ yard (0.4m) of lining fabric
- Glue stick

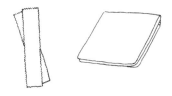

1 PREPARING AND CUTTING FABRICS

From the jelly roll strips cut the following 2½in (6.3cm) squares: five squares for round 1; eight squares for round 2; 16 squares for round 3; 16 squares for round 4; 16 squares for round 5; 16 squares for round 6; 32 squares for round 7; 32 squares for round 8; 32 squares for round 9; 15 squares for round 10; 28 squares for round 11; 12 squares for round 12; and four squares for round 13 (cut this from the remainder of the round 1 or round 2 strip).

From the muslin cut one 14in (35.6cm) square.

From the home décor weight fabric cut: one 14½in (36.8cm) square; two pieces, 4½in x 14½in (11.4cm x 36.8cm); two pieces, 2½in x 11in (6.3cm x 27.9cm); two pieces, 2½in x 14½in (6.3cm x 36.8cm); and two pieces, 2½in x 42in (6.3cm x 106.7cm).

From the lining fabric cut: one piece, 4½in x 6½in (11.4cm x 16.5cm); one piece, 6½in x 14½in (16.5cm x 36.8cm); and two pieces, 2½in x 42in (6.3cm x 106.7cm).

2 PREPARING THE SQUARES

Keep one square from round 1 to one side, and fold all the rest of the squares from all the rounds in half and press.

Fold in each the two sides to form a triangle and press.

3 ASSEMBLING THE BAG FRONT

Round 1: In the centre of the 14in (35.6cm) square of muslin draw an 11in (27.9cm) square. Find the centre of the muslin and the 2½in (6.3cm) square. Place the 2½in square in the very centre of the muslin. A swipe of glue stick will hold the square in place.

Take the four co-ordinating triangles of folded fabric and place them on top of the centre square as per the diagram.

Attach the triangles to the muslin by sewing a seam ⅛in (0.3cm) from the raw edge.

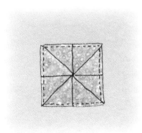

Round 2: Take four triangles from the round 2 pieces and place the points of each of them ½in (1.3cm) from the points of round 1.

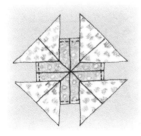

Take the remaining four triangles and place the points of each of them ½in (1.3cm) from the centre.

Attach the triangles to the muslin by sewing a seam ⅛in (0.3cm) from the raw edge.

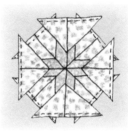

Rounds 3, 4, 5 and 6: Take eight triangles and place the points of each of them ¼in (0.6cm) from the points of the previous round. Take the eight remaining triangles and place them in between the first eight, ensuring that the points are ½in (1.3cm) from the points where the round 2 triangles overlap.

TIP

To ensure that the size is as accurate as possible, make sure that the points of a round are not placed any further than ½in (1.3cm) from the points of the last round.

Add rounds 4, 5 and 6 in the same way, ensuring that you secure the triangles to the muslin by sewing a seam ⅛in (0.3cm) from the raw edge after each round.

Once all pieces have been placed, redraw the 11in (27.9cm) square on top of the edge of the triangles. Sew a seam ⅛in (0.3cm) in from the drawn line.

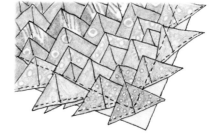

Trim the piece along the drawn line.

Rounds 7, 8 and 9: Take 16 triangles and place the points of each of them ¼in (0.6cm) from the points of the previous round. Take the 16 remaining triangles and place them in between the first 16, ensuring that the points are ½in (1.3cm) from the points where the round 2 triangles overlap or the points of the previous round.

Ensure that you secure the triangles to the muslin by sewing a seam ⅛in (0.3cm) from the raw edge after each round.

Rounds 10, 11, 12 and 13: The remaining four rounds are not true rounds but just make up the corners to take the shape from a circle to a square. Add these in the same way as the full rounds, but instead add to each of the four corners.

Take the two 2½in x 11in (6.3cm x 27.9cm) strips and sew one on to each side of the front panel. Press seams. Take the two 2½in x 14½in (6.3cm x 36.8cm) strips and sew one on to each side of the front panel. Press seams outwards. Topstitch around the front panel.

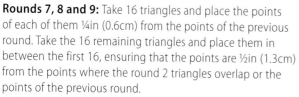

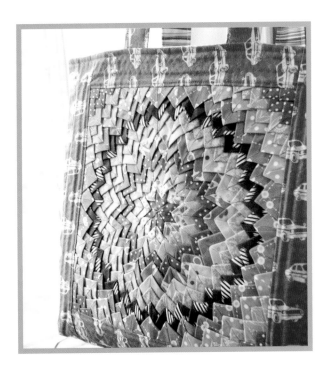

5 ASSEMBLING THE BAG

Take the front panel and, with right sides together, sew one of the 4½in x 14½in (11.4cm x 36.8cm) side panels on to each side, stopping ¼in (0.6cm) from the bottom. Take the back panel and, with right sides together, sew this on to each of the side panels, stopping ¼in (0.6cm) from the bottom. With right sides together, sew in the bottom panel. Turn right sides out.

Repeat these steps for the lining but leaving a 6in (15.2cm) portion of the bottom panel unsewn. Leave inside out.

Place the edges of the handle 3½in (8.9cm) in from the side seams and pin. Secure the handle in place by sewing ⅛in (0.3cm) from the top edge.

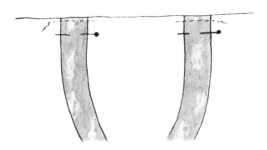

Place the bag inside the lining, align the raw edges and, using a ¼in (0.6cm) seam, sew around the top of the bag.

4 ASSEMBLING THE HANDLES

Take a 2½in x 42in (6.3cm x 106.7cm) strip of bag fabric and a 2½in x 42in (6.3cm x 106.7cm) strip of lining fabric and sew them together down one long edge. Press the seam open.

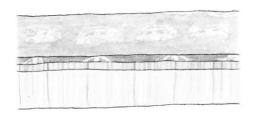

With right sides down, fold in each edge until it meets the edge of the seam allowance and press.

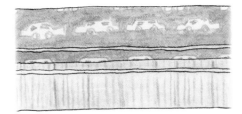

Fold the handle in half down the seam, press and pin. Topstitch the handle ⅛in (0.3cm) down each side. Repeat for the second handle.

6 FINISHING

Turn the whole bag right side out through the hole in the lining. Flatten the top seam. Pin through all layers and topstitch ⅛in (0.3cm) down from the top of the bag. Tuck the raw edges of the hole in the lining and sew the lining closed.

GERBERA BAG CHARM

SIZE: 3⅛in x 4½in
(8cm x 11.4cm)

QUICK and easy to make, this quirky bag charm will give a new lease of life to an old handbag or rucksack. Choose fabric colours either to tone with the bag, or provide a colourful contrast.

YOU WILL NEED

- 1 jelly roll strip
- 2 charm squares
- Scrap of fabric at least 1¾in (4.4cm) square
- Strong thread
- Bag charm lobster clasp
- ¾in (1.9cm) button

1 PREPARING AND CUTTING FABRICS

From the jelly roll strip cut 11 squares, 2½in (6.3cm). From ten of these squares cut ten shapes using template A.
　　From one charm square cut a circle using template B.
　　From the second charm square cut one strip, 2in x 5in (5cm x 12.7cm), for the strap.
　　From the fabric scrap cut one circle using template C.

2 PREPARING THE FLOWER

Fold each flower petal circle in half and press. With strong thread, sew running stitches ⅛in (0.3cm) from the raw edge from one flat side to the other. Pull the flower petals up tightly. Repeat for the remaining nine petals so that you have ten in total. Sew through all ten petals and pull them in tightly to form the flower. Stitch to secure.

3 MAKING THE YOYO

Take the circle cut from template B and place right side down. Fold the edge in by ¼in (0.6cm) and, as you do so, sew a running stitch all around the circle using strong thread.

When you have stitched all the way around the circle, pull the thread tightly so that the edges gather into the centre. Stitch to secure in the centre.

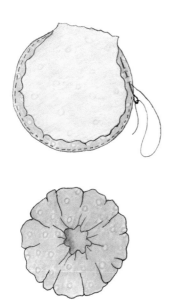

4 MAKING THE STRAP

Fold the strap piece in half with right sides together and sew a seam ¼in (0.6cm) down the long edge. Turn right sides out, press flat and topstitch ⅛in (0.3cm) from each edge.

Take the lobster clasp and thread the strap through the bottom of the clasp. Align the raw edges together and sew on to the back of the flower.

5 COVERING THE BUTTON

Take the circle cut from template B and, using the strong thread, sew a running stitch approximately ¼in (0.6cm) long all around the edge. Pull the thread to gather slightly and then insert the button. Pull the threads tightly and secure.

Sew the button into the centre of the yoyo, then stitch the yoyo down to the front of the flower.

6 FINISHING

Take the circle cut from template C and, using the strong thread, sew a running stitch approximately ¼in (0.6cm) long all around the edge. Pull the thread to gather slightly and then insert the plastic template A that was used to cut the flower petals. Pull the threads tightly and secure leaving the plastic template inside. Stitch to the back of the flower.

TEMPLATES
Shown at 100%

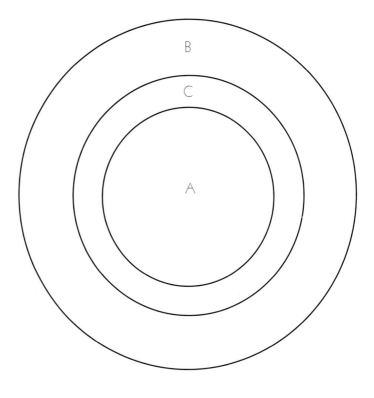

FAIRYTALE PINS'N'THINGS

SIZE: 5¼in x 9in x 3⅛in
(13.3cm x 22.9cm x 7.9cm)

THIS pretty project uses pre-cut charm squares to create a simple yet decorative sewing accessory. Place it on a table or shelf near your work to avoid the problems of dropped pins and scattered loose threads.

YOU WILL NEED

- 1 mini charm pack (40 squares)

- 2 pieces of muslin or scrap fabric at least 4½in x 6½in (11.4cm x 16.5cm)

- 1 fat eighth for lining and pincushion base

- 1 fat eighth of medium-weight fusible interfacing

- Small quantity of play sand

- ⅓ yard (0.3m) of polyester boning, ½in (1.3cm) wide

- Masking tape

1 PREPARING AND CUTTING FABRICS

From the interfacing cut one piece, 4½in x 6½in (11.4cm x 16.5cm) and one piece, 8½in x 14½in (21.6cm x 36.8cm).

From the lining fabric cut one piece, 4½in x 6 ½in (11.4cm x 16.5cm) and one piece, 6½in x 14½in (16.5cm x 36.8cm).

From the polyester boning cut one strip, 14in (35.6cm) long.

From the muslin cut two pieces, 4½in x 6½in (11.4cm x 16.5cm).

2 PREPARING THE THREAD CATCHER PIECE

Take 28 mini charm squares and lay them out seven squares across and four squares down. Once you are happy with the placement, sew these together into rows, and then join the rows together. Press seams open as you go along.

Iron the larger piece of interfacing on to the back of the thread catcher piece. If required, trim to 8½in x 14½in (21.6cm x 35.6cm).

3 PREPARING THE PINCUSHION PIECE

Take six mini charm squares and lay them out three squares across and two squares down. Once you are happy with the placement, sew these together into rows, and then join the rows together. Press seams open as you go along.

Iron the smaller piece of interfacing on to the back of the pincushion piece. If necessary, trim to 4½in x 6½in (11.4cm x 16.5cm).

To make the tabs that attach the pincushion to the thread catcher, take two mini charm squares. Fold these in half and sew down the raw edge using a ¼in (0.6cm) seam. Turn the tabs right side out using a safety pin and flatten so that the seam runs down the centre of each strip. Press flat.

TIP
Substitute fancy printed or embroidered ribbons for the tabs. There are some amazing embroidered ribbons and cotton tapes available.

4 MAKING THE PINCUSHION

Take the stitched pincushion piece and place the edges of the tabs about 1in (2.5cm) from the edge of the top. Sew them ⅛in (0.3cm) from the edge to hold them in place.

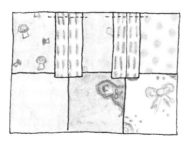

Place the smaller piece of lining fabric on top of the pincushion piece, right sides together so the tabs are sandwiched in between. Using a ¼in (0.6cm) seam allowance, and making sure that the ends of the tabs are tucked in, sew around the edge of the piece leaving a 3in (7.6cm) opening at one end. Turn the pincushion right sides out.

5 MAKING THE THREAD CATCHER

Take the stitched thread catcher piece (see step 1) and fold it in half lengthways, right sides together. Sew a ¼in (0.6cm) seam down the edge. Press the seam open. Lay the piece down and flatten with the seam running down the centre. Sew up the bottom edge with a ¼in (0.6cm) seam. To square the bottom corners of the thread catcher bag, flatten the corners, pin and draw a line 1½in (3.8cm) from the point (see the diagram).

Trim off the excess fabric. Turn the bag right side out. Repeat this step for the larger lining fabric piece but leave approximately 3in (7.6cm) of the bottom seam unstitched, and do not turn the bag right side out.

TIP

This design can readily be adapted to make a larger work bag in which you can store quilting work in progress. Simply scale up the fabric measurements to suit. Alternatively, you could add useful patch pockets to the outside of the thread catcher before you sew it up into a bag.

6 ASSEMBLY

Place the pincushion on the top of the thread catcher bag with the wrong side of the tabs facing the right side of the bag (see the diagram). Pin the tabs to the bag with the inside edges of each tab approximately ½in (1.3cm) from the back seam. Sew a seam ⅛in (0.3cm) from the edge to hold the tabs in place.

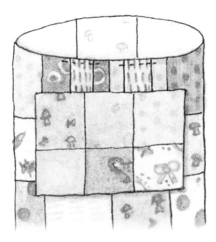

Put the thread catcher bag inside the lining so that the two rights sides are facing each other. Pin together so that the back seams of each piece match each other. Sew all the way around the top ¼in (0.6cm) from the edge.

Take the two muslin pieces and place them on top of each other. Sew around the edge ¼in (0.6cm) from the edge leaving part of one end open. Fill the bag quite firmly with play sand and stitch the opening closed. Gently insert the pincushion inner into the pincushion. It should be a tight fit so be gentle. Then stitch the pincushion opening closed.

TIP

Sand is great to use as a pincushion filling as it help to keep your pins and needles sharp and the weight is great for holding your pincushion on your sewing table. Other alternatives you could use are wool, as the lanolin helps prevent rusting, or even crushed walnut shells.

7 FINISHING

Turn the thread catcher bag right side out through the hole in the bottom of the lining. Flatten the seam. Pin through all layers to hold in place and topstitch around the top of the bag ⅛in (0.3cm) down from the edge.

Tape the ends of the polyester boning together using masking tape. Insert it through the hole and in the lining and manipulate the ring so that it lies at the very top of the thread catcher between the lining and the outside piece; you will find that this is easy to do as the polyester boning is quite flexible. Pin just below it to hold it in place. Stitch just below the boning to form a channel. Fold the thread catcher bag in half so that a crease is formed at each side and so that the boning forms an oval shape. Tuck the raw edges of the hole inside and sew the bottom seam of the lining closed.

YOYO LANYARD AND CARD HOLDER

SIZE: 2¼in x 23in
(5.7cm x 58.4cm)

REPLACE your workplace lanyard with this decorative jelly roll version which is quick and easy to make. Charm squares are used to create yoyo flowers which are then glued to your card holder.

YOU WILL NEED

- 1 jelly roll strip
- 2 charm squares
- Decorative button
- Retractable card holder with carabiner top
- Rigid swipe card holder
- Very strong multi-surface glue
- Compass

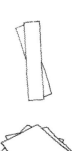

1 MAKING THE LANYARD

Fold the jelly roll strip in half with right sides together. Sew down the length of the jelly roll using a ¼in (0.6cm) seam. Using a safety pin, turn the fabric tube the right way out. Press the tube so the seam runs down the middle.

Lay the lanyard out with both ends the right way up and the seam running down the back off each end, and overlap the ends. Ensure the strip is not twisted.

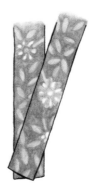

Place the ends together so the seam is on the outside of the top piece and on the inside of the bottom piece. Sew a seam ¼in (0.6cm) from the end, backstitching at each end.

Turn the strip back the right way around so the raw ends and the seam are on the inside. Sew a seam ½in (1.3cm) from the end to enclose the raw ends and again backstitch at each end.

2 MAKING THE FLOWER

On one of the two charm squares draw a 4½in (11.4cm) circle using a compass. On the other charm square draw a 3½in (8.9cm) circle. Cut out the shapes along the drawn lines.

To make the yoyos, turn over the large circle so that the wrong side is facing. Using a double thickness of thread, sew a running stitch ¼in (0.6cm) long all around the edge, folding the edge in by ¼in (0.6cm) as you go.

When you have stitched all the way around the circle, pull the thread tightly so that the edges gather into the centre. Stitch to secure in the centre.

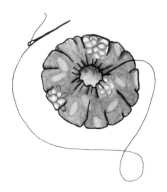

Complete the smaller yoyo in the same way.

3 ASSEMBLY

Layer the two yoyos on top of each other. Sew them together securely through the centre. Then sew the decorative button in the centre. Glue the yoyo flower into the middle of the retractable card holder or rigid swipe card holder using strong glue, and slip the lanyard on to the carabiner loop.

HEXAGON FLOWERS NOTEBOOK

SIZE: 7in x 8½in
(17.8cm x 21.6cm)

ADD a bit of class and distinction to your stitching notebook with this stylish fabric cover embellished with a decorative hexagon design. This project is made using English paper piecing, a traditional method of patchwork which is simple and fun to do.

YOU WILL NEED

- 2 charm squares for flowers
- Fabric scraps for flower centres
- 1 fat quarter for background
- 1 layer cake square for background of flowers
- 1 piece of heavy fusible interfacing at least 10in x 14½in (25.4cm x 36.8cm)
- 1 A5 wire-bound notebook (around 200-250 pages)

  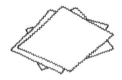

1 PREPARING AND CUTTING FABRICS

From the fat quarter cut two pieces, 9in x 14¼in (24.1cm x 36.8cm); and two pieces, 3½in x 9½in (8.9cm x 24.1cm).
   From the layer cake square cut 12 squares, 2in x 2in (5.1cm x 5.1cm).
   From each of the two charm squares cut six squares, 1½in x 1½in (3.8cm x 3.8cm).
   From each of two small fabric scraps cut one square, 2in x 2in (5.1cm x 5.1cm).
   From the fusible interfacing cut one piece, 9½in x 14¼in (24.1cm x 36.8cm).

2 PREPARING THE PAPER PIECES

Copy the hexagon templates and cut out 14 paper hexagons from both the 1in (2.5cm) and the ¾in (1.9cm) sizes.

3 CONSTRUCTING THE FLOWERS

You will need two flowers in total and for each flower you will need six 1in (2.5cm) hexagons of flower background fabric; six ¾in (1.9cm) hexagons of flower fabric; and one 1in (2.5cm) flower centre.

Tack (baste) all fabric pieces on to the paper templates (see English Paper Piecing). Arrange and hand sew the background pieces together following the diagram, ensuring that the edges of the pieces are lined up as accurately as possible. Complete both flowers in this way.

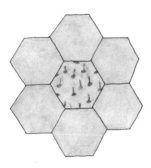

Press the flowers and the ¾in (1.9cm) hexagons and carefully remove all the papers. In the centre of each of the background hexagons place a ¾in (1.9cm) hexagon and pin in place. Appliqué the hexagons in place on both flowers. Sew the two flowers together along one of the flower edges.

4 ATTACHING THE FLOWERS

Fold the outside background piece in half and place the flowers in the centre using your ruler and eye as a guide. Pin securely to the background. Appliqué the flowers in place.

5 ASSEMBLING THE NOTEBOOK COVER

Take the two 3½in x 9½in (8.9cm x 24.1cm) pieces and turn over one long edge on each piece and press. Sew the edge down, about ⅛in (0.3cm) from the edge.

Take one notebook background piece and lay the fusible interfacing piece on top, glue side down. Press until it is adhered completely. If you are using directional fabric, ensure that the correct edges are turned in.

Lay out the background piece with the fusible interfacing on top. Take the two small pieces and lay one face down at each end, ensuring that the turned-over edge is towards the middle of the piece and that the outer edges are aligned.

Place the remaining background piece on top, face down. Ensure that the edges of all three pieces are aligned then pin all three layers together. Sew around the edge using a ¼in (0.6cm) seam. Leave a 4in (10.2cm) gap at the bottom for turning. Trim the excess fabric from the corners and turn right side out. Press.

Press the seam allowance of the unsewn section in, and then sew around the edge ⅛in (0.3cm) from the edge, closing the opening as you go.

Slip the cover on to your notebook and you're ready to go!

TIP

To ensure that the papers stay in position on the fabric while you tack (baste) them, swipe each paper with a glue stick before sticking down on to the fabric, and allow to dry. The papers will still be really easy to remove when the quilt top is complete.

TEMPLATES
Shown at 100%

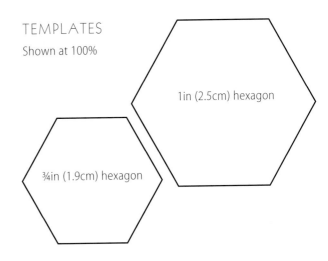

1in (2.5cm) hexagon

¾in (1.9cm) hexagon

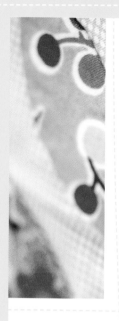

VERDANT SEWING MACHINE COVER

SIZE: 17in x 12in x 8in
(43.2cm x 30.5cm x 20.3cm)

KEEP your sewing machine dust-free by tidying it away under this colourful, leafy fabric cover. This eyecatching project cover combines both patchwork and appliqué.

YOU WILL NEED

- 7 jelly roll strips (2 different light and 5 different medium or dark tones)

- 1 fat quarter for side panels

- Fabric scraps at least 2in (5cm) square

- ½ yard (0.4m) of fabric for lining

- Piece of wadding (batting) at least 20in x 46in (50.8cm x 116.8cm)

- ¾ yard (0.7m) of narrow ricrac

- Small piece of template plastic

- 1 fat eighth heavyweight fusible interfacing

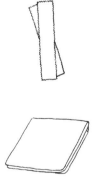

1 PREPARING AND CUTTING FABRICS

From the jelly roll strips choose five medium/dark tones for the main body of the sewing machine cover. Sew these together along their length so that you have a piece measuring 10½in x 42in (26.7cm x 106.7cm).

Also from the jelly roll strips choose two light tone strips for the main body of the sewing machine cover. Sew these together along their length so that you have a piece measuring 4½in x 42in (11.4cm x 106.7cm).

From the pieced medium/dark tone strips cut: two pieces, 17½in (44.4cm); and four strips, 1¾in (4.4cm).

From the pieced light tone strips cut 12 strips, 2½in (6.3cm).

From the fat quarter for the side panels cut two pieces, 8½in x 12in (21.6cm x 30.5cm).

From the fabric scraps cut 24 squares, 2in (5cm).

From the ricrac cut three 9in (22.8cm) lengths.

From the lining fabric cut: one piece, 17½in x 28½in; and two pieces, 8½in x 12in (21.6cm x 30.5cm).

From the wadding (batting) cut: one piece, 20in x 30in (50.8cm x 76.2cm); and two pieces, 10in x 14in (25.4cm x 35.6cm).

2 PREPARING THE LEAVES

Trace the leaf template on to template plastic and cut out. Place the leaf template on to the interfacing and draw around it. You will need 24 of these. Cut them out along the drawn lines.

Iron the leaves on to the back of the fabric scraps, ensuring that there is at least ¼in (0.6cm) all the way around.

Cut away the fabric so that you have about ¼in (0.6cm) of fabric around the leaf, narrowing to around ⅛in (0.3cm) as you get to the corners.

Take the glue stick and apply some glue to each corner. Fold the corners in and stick the fabric down.

Apply the glue stick to the rest of the seam allowance and press the fabric inwards, sticking it to the back of the interfacing. When you turn the leaf over so that the right side is facing you, there should be no raw edges visible.

3 PREPARING THE LEAF PANEL

Take the twelve 2½in (6.3cm) strips and separate them into three groups of four. Arrange them in a checkerboard so that no two squares of the same fabric are next to each other. Sew together using a ¼in (0.6cm) seam and press seams.

Down the centre seam of each piece, on the right side, place a 9in (22.8cm) length of ricrac. Sew a seam down the centre of the ricrac to attach.

Place the leaves on to the panels, ensuring that the points of the leaves are at least ¼in (0.6cm) from the edges. Hand or machine appliqué the leaves down.

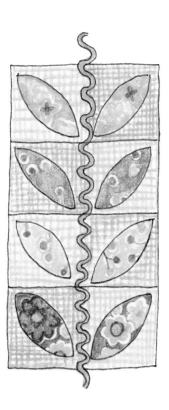

Take the four 1¾in (4.4cm) strips and the leaf pieces and sew them together, alternating between the strips and the leaf panels. Press seams.

4 ASSEMBLING THE MAIN BODY

Take the remaining jelly roll strips, cut them in half and sew one piece to the top and one piece to the bottom of the leaf panel. Press seams.

Sew the leaf panel and the strip panel together down the long edge and press seams. You should now have a piece that measures 17½in x 28½in (44.4cm x 72.4cm).

5 QUILTING

Layer up each of the main body and two side pieces with the wadding (batting) and top and baste using your chosen method. Quilt all pieces as desired and trim to size.

To trim the side panels to the correct shape, first make a mark in the top centre of each of the side panels. Next draw a mark on each side, 3in (7.6cm) from the centre mark.

Lay the ruler against the 3in (7.6cm) mark at the top and the bottom corner of the panel and trim. Do this for each side of each of the two side panels. The top of the side panel should measure 6in (15.2cm) and the bottom 8in (20.3cm). Cut the side panels of the lining in the same way.

TIP

The width of this sewing machine cover can easily be amended if you have a sewing machine with a larger throat length than normal. Simply increase the width of the strips between the leaf panels or increase the width of the side strips.

6 ASSEMBLING THE SEWING MACHINE COVER

Find the centre of the main body and the centre of one of the side pieces, place them right sides together, and pin the pieces together. Sew a ¼in (0.6cm) seam along the top of the side piece, starting ¼in (0.6cm) from one side and finishing ¼in (0.6cm) from the other side.

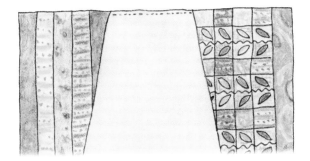

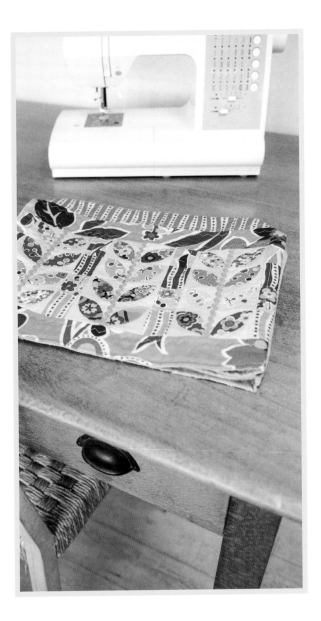

Turn the side piece around and, with right sides together, match the side seams up. Starting from the beginning/end of the previous seam, sew a ¼in (0.6cm) seam down each side of the side panel.

Repeat for the other side to complete the outer piece of the sewing machine cover. Turn right sides out.

Repeat all the above steps for the lining, leaving a 6in (15.2cm) portion of one of the side seams unsewn. Leave the lining inside out. Trim off any excess at the bottom of the side panels.

Put the sewing machine cover inside the lining so that the two right sides are facing each other. Pin so that the side seams of each piece match each other. Sew all the way around the top ¼in (0.6cm) from the edge.

7 FINISHING

Turn the whole thing right side out through the hole in the bottom of the lining. Flatten the top seam. Pin through all layers and topstitch ⅛in (0.3cm) down from the top of the bag. Tuck the raw edges inside and sew the side seam of the lining closed.

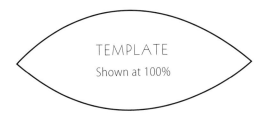

TEMPLATE
Shown at 100%

QUIRKY CUBE BAG

SIZE: 8in x 8in x 13in
(20.3cm x 20.3cm x 33cm)
with a 21in (53.3cm) strap

THIS stylish bag is made from a variety of toning fabrics in black, white and gold using the method of cathedral windows patchwork. Choose colours to match your outfit, or make several bags to wear on different occasions.

1 PREPARING AND CUTTING FABRICS

Cut each of the jelly roll strips in half. Sew the ten jelly roll strips together along their length so that you have a piece measuring 20½in x 21in (52cm x 53.3cm). Press seams.

From the jelly roll strip piece cut six pieces, 2½in x 20½in (6.3cm x 52cm).

From the bag fabric cut: four pieces, 6½in x 20½in (16.5cm x 52cm); four pieces, 2½in x 20½in (6.3cm x 52cm); and one piece, 2½in x 42in (6.3cm x 106.7cm).

From the lining fabric cut: four pieces, 6½in x 20½in (6.3cm x 52cm); and one piece, 2½in x 42in (6.3cm x 106.7cm).

From the wadding (batting) cut four pieces at least 9in x 23in (22.9cm x 58.4cm).

2 ASSEMBLING THE PANELS

Take two 2½in x 20½in (6.3cm x 52cm) bag pieces. Fold in half widthways and press.

Take one 2½in x 20½in (6.3cm x 52cm) strip cut from the jelly rolls and lay the two folded bag pieces on top with the folded edges touching and the raw edges of all layers aligned. Sew a seam ⅛in (0.3cm) down each edge. On to each side, sew a strip cut from the jelly rolls. Press seams.

Using co-ordinating thread, tack (baste) the folded edges together at 2in (5cm) intervals.

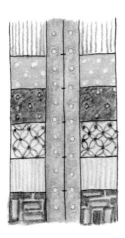

TIP

For greater decoration, use a contrasting thread to stitch down the folded-back edges of the centre panel.

Fold the unsewn edges back around as far as you can without distorting the shape of the piece and appliqué them down, so that the fabric underneath is visible. Repeat this for both panels.

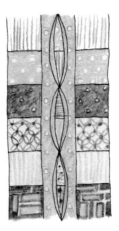

3 ASSEMBLING THE PANELS

Layer up the panels and the 6½in x 20½in bag pieces with the wadding (batting) and lightly quilt.

4 ASSEMBLING THE BAG

Lay out the outer pieces as per the diagram and join together using a ¼in (0.6cm) seam.

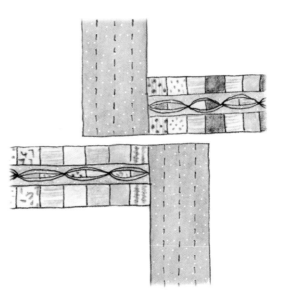

Turn the side pieces aligning the side seams. Then, starting from the end of the bottom seam, sew a ¼in (0.6cm) seam down each side of the side panel.

Repeat for all four sides until the bag forms a cube.

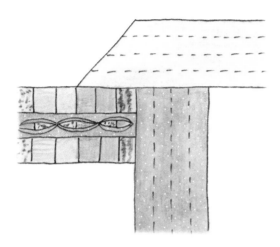

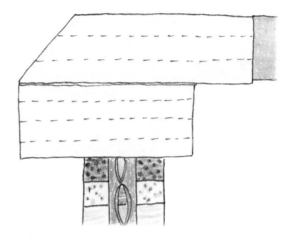

Repeat all above steps for the lining but reverse the direction of the pieces and leave a 6in (15.2cm) portion of one of the side seams unsewn. Leave the lining inside out.

5 ASSEMBLING THE BAG HANDLES

Take a 2½in x 42in (6.3cm x 106.7cm) strip of bag fabric and a 2½in x 42in (6.3cm x 106.7cm) strip of lining fabric and sew them together down one long edge. Press the seam open.

With right sides down, fold in each edge until it meets the edge of the seam allowance and press. Fold the handle in half down the seam, press and pin. Topstitch the handle ⅛in (0.3cm) down each side. Cut the piece in half.

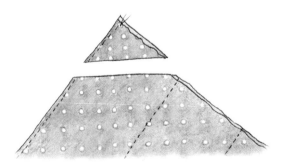

6 ASSEMBLING THE BAG

Lay one of the top corners of one of the bag pieces on the cutting mat so that the raw edge is aligned with the cutting mat lines. Lay your ruler across the top, lining it up with the 1½in (3.8cm) mark. Trim off the corner.

Repeat this for the other three top corners of the bag and the top four corners of the lining.

Place the edges of the handle in the centre of each straight corner edge and pin. Secure the handle in place by sewing ⅛in (0.3cm) from the top edge.

Put the bag inside the lining so that the two right sides are facing each other. Pin so that the side seams of each piece match each other. Sew all the way around the top ¼in (0.6cm) from the edge. Clip the seams at the bottom of where each panel meets.

7 FINISHING

Turn the whole thing right side out through the hole in the bottom of the lining. Flatten the top seam. Pin through all layers and topstitch ⅛in (0.6cm) down from the top of the bag. Tuck the raw edges inside and sew the side seam of the lining closed.

CHEERFUL CARRIER

SIZE: 20in x 26in
(50.8cm x 66cm) with a
22in (55.9cm) strap

CREATE this funky carrier to transport your cutting mat and fabrics. Made from patchwork blocks set at different angles on the background fabric, this design creates a suggestion of movement and flow.

- 1 charm pack (40 squares)

- 1¼ yards (1.1m) of background fabric

- ¾ yard (0.7m) of lining fabric

- ⅔ yards (0.6m) of wadding (batting)

- ¼ yard (0.2m) of fusible web, 35in (88.9cm) wide

1 PREPARING AND CUTTING FABRICS

From the background fabric cut: 40 pieces, 1¼in x 5in (3.2cm x 12.7cm); 40 pieces, 1¼in x 6½in (3.2cm x 16.5cm); two pieces, 1in x 20½in (2.5cm x 52cm); two pieces, 1in x 26½in (2.5cm x 67.3cm); and one piece, 21in x 26½in (53.3cm x 67.3cm).

From the fusible web cut 20 pieces, 3in (7.6cm) square.

From the lining fabric cut: two pieces, 21in x 26½in (53.3cm x 67.3cm); and one piece, 3in x 42in (7.6cm x 106.7cm).

From the wadding (batting) cut: two pieces, 24in x 30in (61cm x 76.2cm); and two pieces, 1¼in x 22in (3.2cm x 55.9cm).

2 PREPARING THE FLOWERS

Following the manufacturer's instructions, press the fusible web squares paper side up on to the back of 20 charm squares. Using the template, draw the flowers on to the paper side of the fusible web.

Cut all flowers out following the drawn lines. You should have 20 flowers in total.

3 PREPARING THE BLOCKS

Take 20 charm squares and on to each one randomly place a flower, ensuring that it is placed at least ¼in (0.6cm) from all edges. Once you are happy with the placement, press to adhere the flowers to the charm squares.

Sew around each flower ⅛in (0.3cm) from the raw edge of the flower to attach it to the base fabric.

Take two 1¼in x 5in (3.2cm x 12.7cm) strips and sew one to each side of the square. Press seams outwards.

Take two 1¼in x 6½in (3.2cm x 16.5cm) strips and sew one to the top and bottom of the squares. Press seams outwards.

TIP

If you prefer and to save time, you could omit the step where you sew around the flowers before quilting, and instead stitch around them as you quilt the bag.

Lay each block on your cutting mat and, following the diagram, make a cut along one side of the block.

Trim each block to 5½in (14cm).

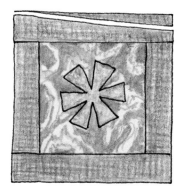

4 ASSEMBLING THE FRONT

Lay the blocks out in four rows of five until you are happy with the placement. Sew each strip of blocks together and press seams open to reduce bulk. Once each row is joined, sew the rows together until the quilt top is complete. Press the seams open as you go along.

Take the two 1in x 20½in (2.5cm x 52cm) pieces and sew them to the top and bottom. Press seams outwards.

Then take the two 1in x 26½in (2.5cm x 67.3cm) pieces and sew them to each side. Press seams outwards.

5 QUILTING

Layer up the backing, wadding (batting) and top and quilt using your chosen method. Repeat for the bag back and wadding (batting). Start your quilting from the centre and work your way out to the edges. Trim both pieces to 21in x 26½in (53.3cm x 67.3cm).

6 ASSEMBLING THE HANDLES

Take a 3in x 22in (7.6cm x 55.9cm) strip of bag fabric. Fold in each edge ¼in (0.6cm) and press.

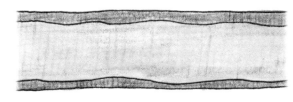

Fold the handle in half and press. Insert a 1¼in (3.2cm) strip of wadding (batting) and topstitch the handle ⅛in (0.3cm) down each side. Repeat for the second handle.

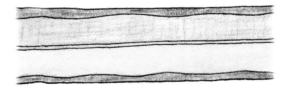

7 ASSEMBLING THE BAG

Take the front and back panels and, with right sides together, sew around three sides. Repeat this for the lining, leaving a 6in (15.2cm) portion of the bottom panel unsewn. Leave inside out.

Place the edges of the handle 7½in (19cm) in from the side seams and pin. Secure the handle in place by sewing ⅛in (0.3cm) from the top edge.

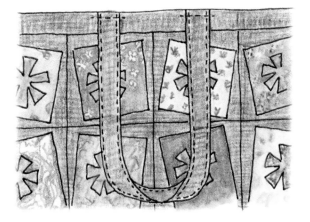

TIP
Just in case you plan to carry multiple mats, rulers and other materials in your bag, stitch across the ends of the handles two or three times to ensure that the handles are securely attached to the bag.

8 FINISHING

Place the bag inside the lining, align the raw edges at the top and, using a ¼in (0.6cm) seam, sew around the top of the bag. Turn the bag right sides out through the unsewn section in the lining.

Flatten the top seam. Pin through all layers and topstitch ⅛in (0.3cm) down from the top of the bag. Tuck the raw edges of the hole in the lining and sew the lining closed.

TEMPLATE
Shown at 100%

MATERIALS AND TECHNIQUES

CUTTING

For cutting background fabrics, making your own pre-cuts, and cutting pieced sections in some of the projects, the most efficient and accurate way of cutting is with a self-healing cutting mat and rotary cutter. Always make sure your blade is sharp, that you always cut away from yourself and that your fingers are well clear of the cutting line!

CUTTING FABRICS

When cutting fabrics it is important that you press your fabrics so that they are nice and flat. The second most important step is to square up your fabric. To do this, fold your fabric so that the selvages are aligned with each other. Line up the folded edge with one of the vertical lines on your cutting mat and, using a long ruler lined up with the markings on your mat, hold the ruler in place and with your rotary cutter cut across the top. You can check that this line is straight by opening the fabric and checking where the fold is that the line is straight and not V-shaped.

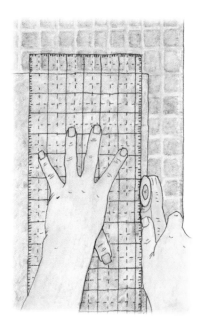

Cutting strip-pieced sections

A number of projects in this book involve cutting strip-pieced sections down into smaller pieces. Cutting your fabrics so that the edges are square to each other is really important when doing this. Use the lines on your cutting mat and your ruler as a guide to ensure that all edges are square to each other.

Cutting with speciality rulers

There are two speciality rulers used in this book: the 22-degree wedge ruler and the quick curve ruler. Specific cutting instructions are detailed in the individual patterns but ensure that the marks on the rulers are correctly lined up with the edges of the fabric to ensure that the pieces are cut as accurately as possible.

CUTTING TEMPLATES

To cut templates for the patterns in this book, simply take your transparent or opaque template plastic and trace the templates with a fine permanent marker, making sure that they are traced as accurately as possible. Cut out the templates using a pair of sharp scissors.

FUSSY CUTTING

Choosing a pattern and then choosing fabrics that fit that design can be challenging but great fun as there are a couple of different options. You can either choose a motif that is approximately the size you need, choose one that is smaller and centre it in your fabric piece, or choose one that is larger and select an area of the motif that you wish to use.

USING A RULER

The square pieces in the centre of the churn dash blocks on the Dasher Bathmat have been fussy cut using this method. The geometric nature of the flower made cutting by ruler the best choice.

1. Find the centre line of the geometric pattern. Then divide the size of the piece you need by two. For example, for the Dasher Bathmat you need a 2½in (6.3cm) square, then half of that would be 1¼in (3.2cm). (If you need a 3½in (8.9cm) square, half of that would be 1¾in (4.4cm).)

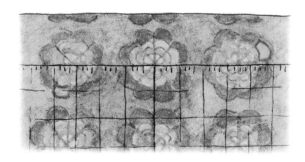

2. Lay your ruler with the 1¼in (3.2cm) line on your ruler on the centre of the design and cut. Turn the fabric around and cut the strip at 2½in (6.3cm) wide or 1¼in (3.2cm) from the centre line again. Cut across the width using the same method.

USING TEMPLATES

1. To make a template, draw or trace the piece size on to clear or opaque template plastic and then add ¼in (0.6cm) all around for the seam allowance. Mark the template with permanent marker or pencil so that you can position the template on the fabric in exactly the same place every time. The way you mark the template is not important so long as it gives you a reference point, such as drawing around the outline of the motif or picking out a feature of the motif as the reference point.

2. Once you have created the template, lay the template on to the fabric, ensuring that the marked lines correspond with the print on the fabric. When you are happy with the placement, draw around the template with your usual marking tools and cut the piece out.

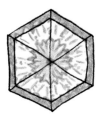 

FABRIC CALCULATIONS FOR FUSSY CUTTING

As fussy cutting requires cutting out the motifs and discarding the rest of the piece, fabric calculations differ from the way you would usually calculate fabric requirements. You need to ensure that you buy enough fabric to allow you to cut the required number of motifs.

MACHINE PIECING

All the projects in this book use a ¼in (0.6cm) seam allowance. Sewing an accurate seam makes all the difference in getting your points and seams to match up, and getting your quilts as perfect as they can be.

Some of the sewing machines designed for quilting provide ¼in (0.6cm) feet as standard but if yours doesn't then for the majority of sewing machines you can buy a ¼in (0.6cm) foot. Some are simply ¼in (0.6cm) wide so this requires you to line up the edge of the fabric with the edge of the foot, but they are also available with the guide down the right-hand side for you to butt the edge of your fabric up to.

It is always best to test your ¼in (0.6cm) by sewing a seam with your ¼in (0.6cm) foot and then measuring it accurately with a ruler. All machines vary slightly so by testing the seam first you can then compensate for this when you are sewing.

STRIP PIECING

Many of the projects in the book, particularly the jelly roll projects, require you to strip piece. To do this, lay your jelly roll strips right sides together with the edges aligned and sew a ¼in (0.6cm) seam all the way down the length, ensuring that your seam is straight and accurate.

Pressing is also the key to the success of strip piecing as your seam lines need to be nice and straight. I find that pressing the seams open prevents the lines from being distorted during pressing.

HALF-SQUARE TRIANGLES

Half-square triangles are particularly common in many quilts and are included in a few projects in this book. This is a great way of making multiple half-square triangles as it avoids having to sew two bias edges together. Fabric is more prone to stretching when sewing on the bias (cross grain) so this method helps keep the fabric stable while sewing.

1. Take the two fabrics that you wish to use for your half-square triangle and lay them on top of each other so that all the raw edges are aligned. Using a ruler and pencil/marking pen, draw a line diagonally across the square from one corner to the other.

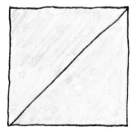

2. Using your ¼in (0.6cm) foot, sew a seam ¼in (0.6cm) away from the drawn line on each side.

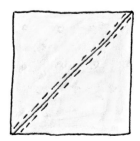

3. Cut down the line, open the two pieces, press and trim them to the required size.

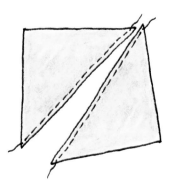

4. Stitch together two triangles from different squares along the stitched lines.

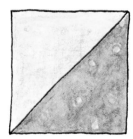

Note: to ensure that your finished pieces are the correct size, make sure that the squares you start with are 1in (2.5cm) larger that the finished size you need. For example, if you need half-square triangles that are 4in (10.2cm) once sewn together, you will need both your squares to start out as 5in (12.7cm).

ENGLISH PAPER PIECING

English paper piecing is an old technique where paper pieces are wrapped in fabric and then sewn together. For this you need: paper templates, needles, contrasting thread for quilting and co-ordinating thread for sewing the pieces together. A glue stick may also be useful.

1. Cut out your paper templates as accurately as possible. Take the fabric pieces and place the template in the centre of the fabrics so that there is at least ¼in (0.6cm) all around the paper template. The English paper piecing patterns in this book all use squares of fabric so on some edges you will have way more than a ¼in (0.6cm) seam allowance. Whether you trim this excess off is optional. Hold the paper in place with either a pin or a swipe of glue stick.

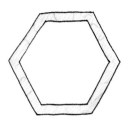

2. Thread your sewing needle with contrasting thread and knot the end. With the back facing, fold down one edge over and about one-third of the way from the right side and push your needle through all the layers to the front and pull through. Bring your needle to the back again.

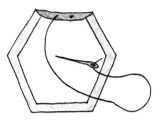

3. At the corner, fold the corner of the second side down over the top of the fabric for the first side and sew a couple of stitches to hold the fold in place. Do not sew through the papers as this will make the papers easier to remove later.

Continue all the way around the shape until you have completed all corners and cut the thread off leaving a 1–2in (2.5–5cm) tail. It is not necessary to tie off.

Note: It is only necessary to take the thread through to the front for any edge longer than around 1½in (3.8cm). For the hexagons for the notebook, just sew the fabric for the corners as above and omit the stitches that go through to the front. That will be sufficient to hold the papers in place until you have finished sewing the flowers together.

4. Place your shapes right sides together with the edge accurately aligned. Double stitch the very corner to make sure it is secure, whip stitch down the edge with stitches approximately ⅛in (0.3cm) apart. Double stitch the end and tie off securely.

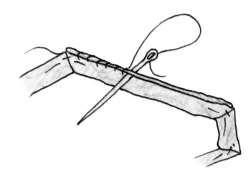

Once your patchwork is complete or all edges have been secured to another piece, snip the threads on the surface and gently pull the paper pieces out. The threads will automatically be pulled through to the back.

PAPER FOUNDATION PIECING

Foundation piecing is an increasingly popular technique where fabric pieces for a block are sewn on to a paper foundation. This method is helpful for piecing small pieces, sharp points or unusual shapes and increases the accuracy of your piecing. Once the block is stitched and trimmed, the paper foundation is torn away. This method can also be used with fine muslin as a base, which is then left in place.

1. Photocopy the template on to printer paper and roughly trim around the edges.

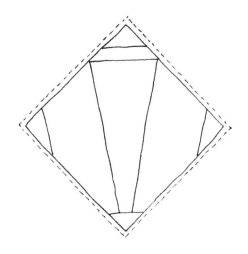

Reduce the stitch length on your sewing machine to 1.5. This is important to make it easier for you to remove the paper later.

2. Turn the paper foundation face down and lay the first piece of fabric on to the paper right side up.

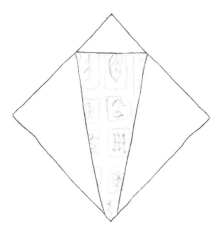

Hold it up to the light and check that the fabric piece overlaps the outside lines by at least ¼in (0.6cm).

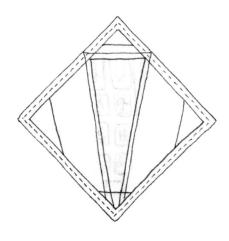

TIP
A swipe of glue stick or a pin will help keep this in place until it is sewn down.

4. Repeat this for all pieces in the order specified in the pattern, making sure that each piece covers the required area and extends ¼in (0.6cm) beyond the edges of the pattern on to the seam allowance.

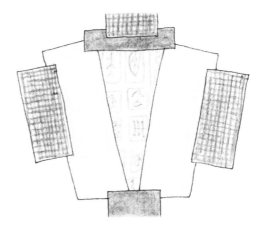

5. Trim the edge of the block along the outer lines and carefully remove the papers. The sewn lines will have perforated the papers so that they are easier to remove.

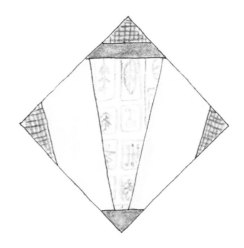

3. Take the second piece of fabric and line it up with the first fabric piece right side down so that it overlaps the dividing line for the first piece by at least ¼in (0.6cm). Check that when you flip the piece back it covers the required area. Carefully turn the whole piece over, holding the fabric in place and sew down the line. Turn back over, flip the second fabric piece back and carefully press the seam open.

PRESSING

To get your piecing as precise as possible, it is important to press your seams as you go along. 'Ironing' the seams using a forward and backwards motion in the same way you would iron a shirt can distort the fabrics and push your seam out of shape. Instead, ensure that you 'press' your seams by lifting the iron up and down on to the area you wish to press. Press the seam on the back first and then turn over and press the front. Quilting convention quite often suggests not using steam, but I find that using steam gets my seams really nice and flat.

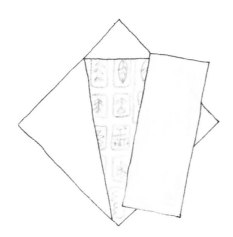

APPLIQUE

Appliqué technique is where you fix a smaller piece of fabric on to a larger piece. There are a few projects in this book that use appliqué and use one of these two following techniques.

HAND APPLIQUE

Hand appliqué is the process where you stitch the smaller pieces down and the stitching is not visible. For this you need your appliqué pieces, pins, a hand sewing needle and co-ordinating thread.

1. Securely pin the appliqué piece on to the foundation piece. Use the shortest pins you have to prevent the thread getting wrapped around the pins as you sew.

2. Starting at one of the corners, stitch down by running the needle at the back of the foundation and bringing the needle back up and through the very edge of the appliqué. Bring the needle back down after each stitch as close to where the needle came up as possible, and again running the needle at the back and bringing the needle back up and through the very edge of the appliqué. Repeat this all around the edge with stitches that are approximately ⅛in (0.3cm) apart. Tie off to finish.

MACHINE FREE MOTION APPLIQUE

Machine appliqué is the process where you stitch the smaller pieces down by free motion stitching on the surface around each shape and the stitching is visible. This method can be used for both appliqué that has folded and raw edges but has been used in a number of projects in the book with raw edge appliqué. This type of appliqué can be used both before the quilt top is complete or as an integral part of your quilting.

For this you need your appliqué pieces fused to the foundation with fusible web, sewing machine, sewing thread and a free motion quilting or darning foot.

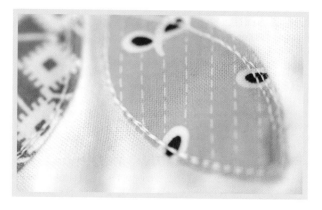

1. Drop the feed dogs on your machine (or replace the foot plate with one that covers your feed dogs depending on your machine) and put on the free motion/darning foot.

2. Put your work under the machine foot. Bring the needle down and back up and pull the bobbin thread up to the surface. Make a couple of stitches in the same place to secure the ends and then bring your needle back down.

3. Start sewing and move your work so that you are sewing about ⅛in (0.3cm) from the edge of your appliqué. It can take some practice to get really good control and the key is getting the machine speed and the speed you move the work to one that suits you. I find that the faster the machine and the faster I move the work, the smoother the lines are.

> ### TIP
> You can alter the effect by sewing more than once around a piece and this is also useful if you have missed the edge of some of your pieces.

LAYERING THE QUILT SANDWICH

Quilts are most commonly made up of three layers: the quilt top, the wadding (batting) and the backing. How the three layers are sandwiched together will determine whether you get wrinkles or puckers in the finished quilt so it is important that you take the time to make the best sandwich possible. The most successful quilt sandwiches are those where all three layers are smoothed out and at the same tension.

To layer the quilt sandwich you need: the quilt top, fabric for backing, wadding (batting), masking tape and a lot of safety pins.

1. Make a backing that is at least 2in (5cm) larger all the way around the quilt. So, for example, if the quilt is 60in (152.4cm) square, you would need the backing to be at least 64in (162.6cm). Cut the wadding (batting) so that it is around the same size as the backing. Ensure that your quilt top is pressed and that any threads visible on the front are snipped off.

2. Lay the backing fabric right sides down on a smooth floor and smooth out wrinkles and creases. Secure the backing to the floor using masking tape at regular intervals. About every 12–18in (30.5–45.7cm) is sufficient. The fabric needs to be taut but avoid stretching it. Secure one side, then the opposite side and then repeat for the remaining two sides.

3. Centre the wadding (batting) on top of the backing, and starting from the centre smooth it out. Centre the quilt on top of the wadding (batting) and backing and again, starting from the centre, smooth it out.

4. Pin all three layers together using safety pins starting from the centre and working outwards. You can either use straight safety pins or you can purchase curved safety pins that are specially designed for this purpose. The rule of thumb is that you should pin at intervals roughly the width of your hand. This may seem excessive but the more pins you use, the better the final result will be. Once you have finishing pinning, gently remove the masking tape and you are ready to quilt.

QUILTING

The purpose of quilting is to secure all three layers of a quilt to each other and prevent the wadding (batting) from bunching up. This can be done either by hand, on a domestic sewing machine or by a professional long-arm quilter.

If quilting on a domestic machine, it is a good idea to roll the areas up that you are not immediately quilting so that the bulk doesn't get in the way while you are sewing. Use as large a table as you can so the weight of the quilt is supported.

STRAIGHT LINE QUILTING

For this you will need the quilt sandwich, a walking or leather foot and quilting thread. A walking foot is the key to success as it feeds the three layers through the machine at the same rate so avoiding puckers in your quilt top.

1. It is best to start your quilting from the centre and work outwards, so find a suitable place to start. Put your quilt sandwich under the machine foot and bring the needle down and back up and pull the bobbin thread up to the surface. Do a couple of small stitches by reducing your stitch length, to secure the ends.

2. Increase the stitch length back to where you want it and start stitching. Stitch from the centre and quilt outwards, removing the safety pins as you go. If you are stitching right to the edge of the quilt, you do not need to secure the ends at the edges, but if you are finishing your line earlier then do a couple of small stitches at the end of the lines of stitching to secure the ends.

FREE MOTION QUILTING

For this you will need your quilt sandwich, a free motion quilting or darning foot and quilting thread.

1. Drop the feed dogs on your machine (or replace the foot plate with one that covers the feed dogs depending on your machine) and put on the free motion/darning foot.

2. Put your quilt sandwich under the machine foot and bring the needle down and back up and pull the bobbin thread up to the surface. Make a couple of stitches in the same place to secure the ends and then bring your needle back down.

3. Start sewing and move your work under the machine. At first it can feel rather strange as essentially it is like writing but by moving the paper rather than the pen! It can take some practice to get good control and the key to success is getting the machine speed and the speed you move the work under the foot to a speed that suits you. I find that the faster the machine and the faster I move the work, the smoother are the lines. Continue quilting, removing the safety pins as you go along.

2. Quilt by making running stiches along the area you wish to quilt, making sure that the stitches go through all three layers of the quilt. To get the line of stitches straight, make as many stitches as possible on your needle before pulling the needle through.

The uniformity of the stitches is more important than their length. Try to keep all the stitches the same length and for the distance between the stitches to be approximately the same size as the stitches.

3. To fasten off, take the thread through to the back of the quilt and sew a couple of tiny stiches to secure. Then run the needle in between the layers and back up 2in (5cm) away and snip off the thread. The end will then be buried in your quilt sandwich.

HAND QUILTING

For this you will need your quilt sandwich, a quilting needle and hand quilting thread or perle cotton. Start your hand quilting in the centre of the quilt and work outwards. You may find it useful to use a quilting hoop.

1. Thread your needle and tie a small knot in the end. Insert the needle into the front of the quilt at an area near where you want to start quilting, and bring the needle back up where you want to start. Pull the thread hard enough so that you pull the knot through to the back of the quilt top, but not hard enough to pull the thread back out. The knot will then be hidden between your quilt sandwich layers. Make a couple of small stitches to secure the thread.

PROFESSIONAL QUILTING

If you aren't feeling brave enough to have a go at your own quilting, you could always take your quilt to a professional long-arm quilter who can quilt it for you. You simply provide them with your quilt top and backing piece, choose your quilting design and they do the rest.

There are two types of quilting that professional quilters do. The first is known as **pantograph patterns.** These are continuous stitched patterns that are quilted all over the surface of the quilt and don't take into account the design elements of the quilt. This is sometimes done freehand by the quilter but more often is done by the machine's computer. These pantograph patterns can include swirls, circles, waves and zigzags.

The second type is **custom quilting** where the quilter takes the design of the quilt into account. This is much more expensive as it involves the quilter designing the quilting using multiple different patterns, and is generally very labour intensive for the quilter. The effects can be amazing though, so this is definitely worth considering for a complex design or when you want certain design elements of the quilt to stand out.

Find a long-arm quilter by asking friends for recommendations or search online. As you will be trusting them with your quilt it is worth looking at their work first, and make sure that the design and the cost are decided up front.

BINDING

For this you will need fabric or jelly roll strips and co-ordinating thread. The binding on a quilt is the final step in completing your quilt and it covers all the raw edges. The two most common forms of binding are straight grain binding and bias binding. Straight grain binding is cut on the straight grain of the fabric and is suitable for quilts with straight/square edges. Bias binding is cut across the stretchy bias of the fabric and is suitable for curved or scalloped edges.

Binding strips are most commonly cut at 2½in (6.3cm) or 2¼in (5.7cm) wide and sometimes narrower depending on the quilting project and the width of binding you require. All quilts in this book use 2½in (6.3cm) straight grain binding.

1. Trim your quilt around the edge and then measure around the edge of the whole quilt and add about 10in (25.4cm). This is the length of the binding you will need.

2. From your binding fabric, cut enough strips to equal the length you need. If the pattern uses jelly roll strips, then this has already been done for you.

3. Sew the 2½in (6.3cm) strips together end to end until you have one long strip. Press the seams open.

4. Fold the binding strip in half lengthways so that the two raw edges are aligned, and press. Continue down the whole length of the binding strip until all of it has been pressed.

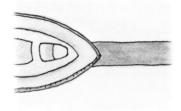

5. Starting about halfway down one of the quilt edges and leaving a 5in (12.7cm) tail, align the edge of the quilt and the edges of the two layers of binding together and sew a seam ¼in (0.6cm) from the edge through all layers. Stop when you get to ¼in (0.6cm) from the edge.

6. On the corner, fold the binding strip away from you at a 90-degree angle and then fold the binding back down so that the fold is on the edge of the quilt and the raw edge of the binding is now aligned with the second edge of the quilt.

7. Starting from the very edge, continue, backstitch and then sew down the edge of the quilt using a ¼in (0.6cm) seam. Repeat this step when you get to every corner until all four corners have been completed.

8. Sew down the last edge until you get to around 6in (15.2cm) from where you started. Backstitch to secure and trim both ends to around 5in (15.2cm).

9. Bring both tails of the binding together and at the mid-point between where the seam started and finished, fold the binding ends back on themselves so that the folds just meet together. Press with your finger or the iron so that the fold lines are clearly visible.

10. Open up the binding pieces, pin the two pieces right sides together along the fold and sew down the fold line. This can be a bit tricky but fold the quilt as necessary to allow you to get the ends under the foot of your sewing machine.

11. Trim the seam allowance to ¼in (0.6cm), press the seams open and re-fold the binding. Sew the last of the binding to the quilt and then you are ready for the hand sewing to finish off.

HAND SEWING THE BINDING

For this you will need a hand sewing needle and co-ordinating thread.

1. Thread your needle and with the thread single, tie a knot in the end. Starting at one corner, fold the binding over to the back of the quilt. If you wish you can pin the binding in place or you could use binding clips or hairclips to keep it in place while you sew.

2. Secure the binding to the back of the quilt by running the needle in between the layers and bringing the needle back up and through the very edge of the binding. Bring the needle back down after each stitch as close to where the needle came up as possible, and again run the needle in between the layers and bring the needle back up and through the very edge of the binding. Repeat this all along the edge with stitches that are ¼–½in (0.6–1.3cm) apart.

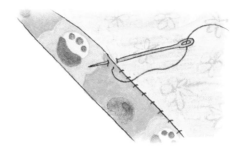

3. When you get to the corners, sew up to the very edge of the quilt and then fold the mitred corner back down. Continue sewing around the quilt until all edges have been stitched down.

RESOURCES

GENERAL QUILTING SUPPLIES

For those of you who are fortunate enough to have quilting shops nearby, you should be able to get most of your basic quilting supplies there and it is great if you can support your local shops. If you live in a quilting wasteland and do not have a suitable shop nearby, all quilting supplies can be bought online. Shop around to find the best prices.

FABRIC AND PRE-CUTS

There are many fabric manufacturers who supply pre-cuts. Some do the full range and others just certain ones. The ones who produce the largest range are Moda and Robert Kaufman but Freespirit, Riley Blake and other quilting fabric manufacturers also now produce them.

For those of you online, an internet search will bring you a host of shops that sell pre-cuts, but don't forget when you are searching that the names of pre-cuts vary between manufacturers. Once you find what you are looking for, it pays to shop around, as the cost can vary massively from shop to shop as do shipping costs.

There are also many quilting shops – both bricks and mortar, and online – that put their own pre-cuts and bundles together. These can provide the most interesting fabric combinations as all fabrics in a pre-cut won't necessarily be from the same line, so ask at your local quilting store to see whether they do. Don't forget that you can also cut your own!

OTHER USEFUL PRODUCTS

There are a couple of specialist rulers used in this book:

- Jenny Pedigo's curved ruler is available at many online stores but can be purchased directly from Jenny at: www.sewkindofwonderful.com
- 22.5 degree rulers are available in a couple of different versions but I recommend the Nifty Notions Cut For The Cure ruler. Not only is it a great ruler but a percentage of the sales also go to the The Chicagoland Affiliate of The Susan G. Komen Breast Cancer Foundation.

The Giant's Causeway quilt is an English paper piecing project that requires a paper template to wrap your fabric around. These can easily be cut by photocopying the templates in the book, stapling them to a couple of additional sheets of printer paper and then cutting them out. There is also a great website from where you can print templates out directly from your computer – www.incompetech.com . If you go to the graph paper section and select the shape you want, you can then specify the size of shape you require and download a PDF. The Giant's Causeway quilt uses 2in (5cm) hexagons and 2in (5cm) squares. You can also buy pre-cut paper shapes at www.paperpieces.com.

INTERNET INSPIRATION

There are mountains of inspiration out there on the internet, without which I wouldn't be quilting at all! Here's a few websites you may find useful:

Fat Quarterly (www.fatquarterly.com)
Fat Quarterly is an e-zine (electronic magazine) for modern stitchers, by stitchers and was started by members of the online modern quilting community. New issues of *Fat Quarterly* are released four times per year and each issue is full of original patterns and project ideas from members of the creative community, features of new fabric lines, articles about developments in the sewing and quilting industry, and interviews. It has a supporting blog so drop in and say Hi!

Flickr (www.flickr.com)
Flickr is an amazing source of inspiration and great for those of you who live in quilting wastelands and have friends and family who don't understand why you are hoarding bits of fabric and constantly have bits of thread stuck to your socks. There is a massive quilting community on Flickr who all post pictures of their amazing sewing/craft projects. There are groups, quilting bees, swaps and quilt-a-longs for you to get involved with and make new friends all over the world.

Quilting Gallery (www.quiltinggallery.com)
Quilting Gallery is a good place to meet thousands of quilters from around the world in the quilting bloggers directory, and browse the quilt shop locator for quilting retailers and professionals. There is a world-wide directory of quilt guilds and a quilter's market area where you can get all the latest on quilting books, patterns and notions.

Sewing Directory (www.sewingdirectory.co.uk)
A great website to find sewing suppliers (both local and online), sewing courses, groups, and general sewing news. It is full of information, inspiration, articles and a great resource for the quilters based in the UK.

Twitter (www.twitter.com)
There is a huge community on Twitter, chatting and posting pictures of their work. It's a great place to see what the craft folks are up to and to get advice quickly. It's fast paced and fun, although beware, it is addictive.

ACKNOWLEDGEMENTS

Writing this book has been a real journey and wouldn't have been possible without many amazing people.

My first thanks go to my precious little boy Jack. He came into our home and our lives like a whirlwind in the spring of 2011 and we will be forever changed by him in the most amazing way. He has taught us so much about ourselves. Everything we do from now is about making the best possible life for him and giving him parents he can be proud of and role models that show him that anything is possible if you love something enough.

Huge thanks also go to my wonderful husband Sandy who supports me in what I love to do. He puts up with soup and toasted sandwiches for tea, threads on all his clothes, quilt tops hung over every door and fabric piled on every flat surface in the house. He rarely moans - unless there's no room to sit down and tie his shoelaces or the piles of fabric extend into the kitchen!

Thanks also to my Mum for instilling the love of fabric in me, and to both Mum and Dad for giving me my first sewing machine and for looking at my newly made quilts and 'oohing' and 'ahhing' at appropriate times.

Many many thanks go to the folks at F&W: Sarah Callard and Ali Myer first and foremost for liking my work enough to ask me to do a book and Heather Haynes for being ultra-patient during the editing process.

Thanks also go to the designers and fabric manufacturers who have supported me with this project:

- Art Gallery Fabrics (www.artgalleryfabrics.com)
- Blend Fabrics (www.blendfabrics.com)
- Robert Kaufman Fabrics (www.robertkaufman.com)
- Michael Miller Fabrics (www.michaelmillerfabrics.com)
- Moda Fabrics (www.unitednotions.com)
- Lu Summers (www.blu-shed.blogspot.com)
- Patty Young (www.modkidboutique.com)

And the most amazing long-arm quilter, Christine Marriage, who has lovingly transformed many of the quilts in this book from nice quilts to amazing heirlooms, often at short notice. I don't know what I would have done without you!

Last, but certainly not least, huge thanks go to the *Fat Quarterly* folks for their patience when I was too busy on Planet Book to have much mental capacity left for anything else. Love you all!

Brioni

ABOUT THE AUTHOR

I live in Leeds, UK, with my husband, a very energetic toddler, my two kitties and pretty much wall-to-wall quilts and fabric! Working full time and being a mum cuts down my sewing time but I do manage to squeeze quilting into just about every waking moment.

I have been sewing on and off for most of my life, which was inevitable being the daughter of a tailor and dressmaker - it's in my genes. My first sewing machine was a Holly Hobby wind-up one that I got one year for Christmas and I would get that out whenever Mum got hers out. I (badly) made handbags and Sindy clothes and was never very satisfied with how they turned out.

I got my first 'grown-up' sewing machine for my 21st birthday while studying for a degree in Textile Design and Technology at Huddersfield University and had marvellous fun sewing bits of knitting, paper, masking tape, lumpy handmade felt and anything else that would fit under the foot. Not surprisingly, that sewing machine is now dead and lives in the great sewing machine graveyard in the sky.

I had been itching to make a patchwork quilt for what seemed like forever and finally I bit the bullet about seven years ago, never imagining that it would suck me in and lead to the biggest obsession I've ever had!

I (infrequently!) blog at www.flossyblossy.blogspot.com and participate in Flickr swaps and quilting bees (as flossyblossy) as often as I can find the time.

In April 2010 I co-founded *Fat Quarterly* which is a quarterly e-zine (electronic magazine) for modern stitchers. The e-zine contains a mix of quilt patterns, small project patterns, articles and design challenges, and in 2011 the *Fat Quarterly* crew released our first book: *The Fat Quarterly Shape Workshop for Quilters*.

Other than published patterns in *Fat Quarterly* and *The Fat Quarterly Book*, my pattern designs have been published in a number of collaborative books and I have taught classes at the Festival of Quilts in Birmingham, at the Fat Quarterly Community Retreats held in London each year and at my local quilt shop, The Skep.

I collect fabric like others collect Lladro figurines and already have more quilts and fabric than I know what to do with, but the more quilts I make the more I *want* to make! I will most likely just stack them up and stroke them!

INDEX

A DAVID & CHARLES BOOK
© F&W Media International, Ltd 2013

David & Charles is an imprint of F&W Media International, Ltd
Brunel House, Forde Close, Newton Abbot, TQ12 4PU, UK

F&W Media International, Ltd is a subsidiary of F+W Media, Inc
10151 Carver Road, Suite #200, Blue Ash, OH 45242, USA

Text and Designs © Brioni Greenberg 2013
Layout and Photography © F&W Media International, Ltd 2013
First published in the UK and USA in 2013. Reprinted in 2014.

A catalogue record for this book is available from the British Library.

ISBN-13: 978-1-4463-0293-4 paperback
ISBN-10: 1-4463-0293-8 paperback

Printed in USA by RR Donnelley for:
F&W Media International, Ltd
Brunel House, Forde Close, Newton Abbot, TQ12 4PU, UK

10 9 8 7 6 5 4 3 2

Acquisitions Editor: Sarah Callard
Editor: Jeni Hennah
Project Editor: Heather Haynes
Senior Designer and Illustrator: Victoria Marks
Photographers: Jack Kirby and Jack Gorman
Senior Production Controller: Kelly Smith

F+W Media publishes high quality books on a wide range of subjects.
For more great book ideas visit: **www.stitchcraftcreate.co.uk**